To Mix With Time .. NEW AND
SELECTED
POEMS . . .

TO
MIX
WITH
TIME

New and Selected Poems

MAY SWENSON

New York

CHARLES SCRIBNER'S SONS

CONTENTS

FROM *A Cage Of Spines*

1

TO MIX WITH TIME 1

···then I saw it flow···

THE UNIVERSE

What
is it about,
the universe
about
us stretching out? We within our brains within it think
we must unspin the laws that spin it. We think
why because
we think
because.
Because
we think
we think
the universe
about
us.
But does it think,
the universe?
Then what
about?
About
us? If not, must there be cause
in the universe?
Must it have laws? And what
if the universe
is *not about*
us? Then what?
What
is it about
and what
about
us?

GOD

They said there was a	Thing
that could not	Change
They could not	Find
it so they	Named
it	God
They had to	Search
so then it must be	There
It had a	Name
It must exist	Somewhere
The	Name
was	God
the	Thing
that could not	Change
They could not	Find
it What is	Lost
is	God
They had to	Search
for what could not be	Found
What can't be	Found
is	Changeless
It is	God
The	Name
is clue The	Thing
is	Lost
	Somewhere
They	Found
the	Name
The	Name
is	Changeless
	God

OUT OF MY HEAD

                        If I could get
          out   of my
          head   and
          into   the
          world.
                        What am I saying?
          Out   of my
          head?
                        Isn't my
          head
            in   the
          world?
            In   it I'm
            in   it, a
          round
          place
            in   a bigger
          round
          place
    someplace.
                        Seems like the
          center.
                        Every
          head
            in   there's a
       center,   it
          thinks.
                        It
          thinks!
                        O.K., let's say I'm
          out   and
            in   the
          round   free
          world:
          Back   there's the tight aluminum sphere
                        I jumped
          out   of, slammed the door like an icebox.
                        A clean landscape
       around   me, an inch or two of "snow"—
                        rock-dust from those

peaks
          in the distance. No colder here,
              even if it is wider. Very few things
around   —just the
peaks.   It'll take weeks to reach them.
              Of course I came here in my
head.

              I'll be taking it
back.

              The idea is to make a vehicle
     out of it.

THE WISH TO ESCAPE
INTO INNER SPACE

All is too open:
all expands, explodes
and scampers out and speeds apart.

What was a ball and solid now balloons,
the outline thin,
the core weightless.

What was full
and held to a pole centrifugal,
what gathered, while it spun, coherent mass,

seized light, shape,
ordered time and motion,
worked upon itself its own proportion:

to be round,
smooth in its orbit,
beautifully closed—

spurts out erratic, widens,
retreats from its core,
feels itself emptied, floats detached . . .

is dragged
through galactic vapors:
the cold pain of unwanted growth.

DOWNWARD

That there were men.
That we are their ghosts.
That men died long ago.

That there was life.
That ours is merely its shadow.

That we have fallen
from a peak on the high past
and are no longer men.

That this is the reason
for our hopelessness,
the reason our life is crippled.

That we grope
upon the slope of the past
and grasp nothing
but our cravings.

Our forward aims
are but our backward looks.
We can barely remember life
for it belonged to *Them*.

LET US PREPARE

to get beyond the organic
for surely there is something else
to which it is an impediment an opaque pod
What if it is sight that blinds
hearing that deafens
touch that makes us numb?
What if trussed in a jacket of blood
to a rack of bone we smother
in the dungeon of our lungs?
Today we are in our brain
a laboratory
Must we be here
tomorrow?
Are there not
pinnacles
on which to stand
cleanly
without a head?
Between the belly
of the sun and the belly
of the world
must we bounce forever
magnetized generations of the circle?
Let us eat nothing but darkness
refuse our stale orbit
and walk only in sleep
there to descry a crack in the future
and work to widen it
Let us prepare to bare ourselves outside the gibbet-hood
of the world
without excuse of flesh or apology of blood

LANDING ON THE MOON

When in the mask of night there shone that cut,
we were riddled. A probe reached down
and stroked some nerve in us,
as if the glint from a wizard's eye, of silver,
slanted out of the mask of the unknown—
pit of riddles, the scratch-marked sky.

When, albino bowl on cloth of jet,
it spilled its virile rays,
our eyes enlarged, our blood reared with the waves.
We craved its secret, but unreachable
it held away from us, chilly and frail.
Distance kept it magnate. Enigma made it white.

When we learned to read it with our rod,
reflected light revealed
a lead mirror, a bruised shield
seamed with scars and shadow-soiled.
A half-faced sycophant, its glitter borrowed,
rode around our throne.

On the moon there shines earth light
as moonlight shines upon the earth . . .
If on its obsidian we set our weightless foot,
and sniff no wind, and lick no rain
and feel no gauze between us and the Fire,
will we trot its grassless skull, sick for the homelike shade?

Naked to the earth-beam we will be,
who have arrived to map an apparition,
who walk upon the forehead of a myth.
Can flesh rub with symbol? If our ball
be iron, and not light, our earliest wish
eclipses. Dare we land upon a dream?

THE SHAPE OF DEATH

What does love look like? We know
the shape of death. Death is a cloud
immense and awesome. At first a lid
is lifted from the eye of light:
there is a clap of sound, a white blossom

belches from the jaw of fright,
a pillared cloud churns from white to gray
like a monstrous brain that bursts and burns,
then turns sickly black, spilling away,
filling the whole sky with ashes of dread;

thickly it wraps, between the clean sea
and the moon, the earth's green head.
Trapped in its cocoon, its choking breath
we know the shape of death:
Death is a cloud.

What does love look like?
Is it a particle, a star—
invisible entirely, beyond the microscope and Palomar?
A dimension unimagined, past the length of hope?
Is it a climate far and fair that we shall never dare

discover? What is its color, and its alchemy?
Is it a jewel in the earth—can it be dug?
Or dredged from the sea? Can it be bought?
Can it be sown and harvested?
Is it a shy beast to be caught?

Death is a cloud,
immense, a clap of sound.
Love is little and not loud.
It nests within each cell, and it
cannot be split.

It is a ray, a seed, a note, a word,
a secret motion of our air and blood.
It is not alien, it is near—
our very skin—
a sheath to keep us pure of fear.

EACH LIKE A LEAF

Each like a leaf
like a wave
to be replaced
repeated

What do we crave
heated by cerebral
fire?

Transitive as flames
that turn
in a furnace
Or sleet falling
separately settling

to one sheet
Forms faced alike
we dance in some
frame

We are a sea
its waves
cannot name
only be

We are a thick
wood
by its leaves made
not understood

As flames their flight
and snow its white
do not perceive
we weave asleep

a body
and awake unravel
the same veins
we travel

THE PRIMITIVE

I walk a path that a mountain crosses.
I am walking toward the mountain.
I have been making the path, I suppose.
Its trace is behind me. I see how it goes
ahead of me also. Perhaps I make it with my eyes.
    Then have I made the mountain also?
More likely the mountain makes itself,
and lets me walk here. Or it lets the path
come upon it. And whatever may be
on the path may approach . . . Why not?
    Or perhaps, thrown out by the mountain once,
like a stone I fell here. Or I fell
in the path farther back, where it already lay.
And then started on my way,
as now, toward the mountain.
    The thing is, I cannot see over the mountain.
It is there, a gradual great rise of the ground.
As I walk, I am crossing it really, already:
the path is rising ever so gently.
But there is the peak. Do I want to go *over* the mountain?

    I see I have come quite far already.
It is strange to look back . . . as if down a thread
with no knot! Before me the path is almost level,
and narrow. But higher, ahead
on the mountain's wedge, it widens. That is strange.
    What would I prefer, then? To stay here,
midway, facing the mountain? To stop,
and not look up or down? Or to drop
back, downwards? I ask myself such things, *while walking!*
—and smile to myself. *Forward, forward is the only choice.*

    But am I sure of this? What if, for instance,
I do make the path with my eyes?
And since it is on the mountain,
I am making the mountain?
There is no one else on this path, after all.
    All the others—although in some way
it is also theirs—this mountain—
their paths make it a separate mountain.

Yet it is mine, in some same parallel way
as I am all the others. I notice this sometimes.
   They are all around me, beside me, walking.
Or within me, when I remember them.
So that they are myself.
So then I am all alone on this mountain?
It must be that I make it. With my eyes?

   I am walking, and talking to myself as I walk—up—
the mountain. I will come to the summit at last.
There are no separate ways about that . . .
Which ought to be a good thing. Except that,
will I know when I reach the peak?
   Will I see *the other side?* I can't "see"
what it may be like—the other side. Except
as being like *this* side . . . No, no,
that would be too foolish! And then,
there is the omen . . . that I shall go blind.
   It is said that this happens
before reaching the peak, so that no one may know
just when he is crossing the mountain.
Then have my eyes, that made this path, that makes
this mountain, made this fate for themselves?

   Oh, eyes, turn and look at me,
instead of always ahead or behind! No, no, no,
such a thing is insane! Mountain, again
you have thrown me back, and down, like a stone!
You are the One! I am yours.
   There is nothing I can know but you.
And I can never know you. Yet we are each other,
are we not? As a pebble is a fraction of the rock
it came from? I must know you, as I know myself.
Exactly that. *But need you know me?*
   Am I not rolling up to you, mountain, as I walk?
Was I "thrown away" upon your self-forgotten body,
and are you now pulling me into your great head again?
Will you let me, finally, see your other side?
Surely some one may see it, sometime?
   What if I, steadfastly, determine
to reach your peak, *without going blind?*

If you can throw me from yourself,
you can take me as quickly up.
Or I will hurry to climb, faithfully, by myself.
   I PROMISE
NEVER
TO TAKE MY EYES
FROM YOUR PEAK.
Mountain, give me a sign!

   No . . . I think, rather, that you do not care.
Perhaps it is a small nobility to think this way . . .
Can pebbles expect a summit?
Enough that we have "eyes"—for a time.
Strange enough. *I cannot understand it.*

NIGHT PRACTICE

I

will

remember

with my breath

to make a mountain,

with my sucked-in breath

a valley, with my pushed-out

breath a mountain. I will make

a valley wider than the whisper, I

will make a higher mountain than the cry;

will with my will breathe a mountain, I will

with my will breathe a valley. I will push out

a mountain, suck in a valley, deeper than the shout

YOU MUST DIE, harder, heavier, sharper, a mountain than

the truth YOU MUST DIE. I will remember. My breath will

make a mountain. My will will remember to will. I, suck-

ing, pushing, I will breathe a valley, I will breathe a mountain.

THE SURFACE

First I saw the surface,
then I saw it flow,
then I saw the underneath.

In gradual light below
I saw a kind of room,
the ceiling was a veil,

a shape swam there
slow, opaque and pale.
I saw enter by a shifting corridor

other blunt bodies
that sank toward the floor.
I tried to follow deeper

with my avid eye.
Something changed the focus:
I saw the sky,

a glass between inverted trees.
Then I saw my face.
I looked until a cloud

flowed over that place.
Now I saw the surface
broad to its rim,

here gleaming, there opaque,
far out, flat and dim.
Then I saw it was an Eye:

I saw the Wink that slid
from underneath the rushes
before it closed its lid.

HOW TO BE OLD

It is easy to be young. (Everybody is,
at first.) It is not easy
to be old. It takes time.
Youth is given; age is achieved.
One must work a magic to mix with time
in order to become old.

Youth is given. One must put it away
like a doll in a closet,
take it out and play with it only
on holidays. One must have many dresses
and dress the doll impeccably
(but not to show the doll, to keep it hidden.)

It is necessary to adore the doll,
to remember it in the dark on the ordinary
days, and every day congratulate
one's aging face in the mirror.

In time one will be very old.
In time, one's life will be accomplished.
And in time, in time, the doll—
like new, though ancient—will be found.

TO MIX WITH TIME 2

···touching his toe···

The poems in Part 2, together with *How To Be Old* in Part 1, are from a group written in France, Italy and Spain. The author is grateful to the Amy Lowell Travelling Scholarship Fund which enabled them to be made.

DEATH INVITED

Death invited to break his horns
on the spread
cloth. To drop his head
on the dragged flag on the sand.
Death's hooves slipping
in blood, and a band
of blood down the black side.
Death's tongue, curved in the open mouth
like a gray horn, dripping
blood. And
six colored agonies decking the summit
of his muscled pride.
Death invited to die.

The head
of death, with bewildered raging eye,
flagged down,
dragged down to the red
cloth on the sand.
Death invited to stand,
legs spread,
on the spot of the cape.
To buckle stubborn knees and lie
down in blood on the silken shape.
Beg blindness come to the sun-pierced eye.

The sword, sunk at the top of the shoulder's pride—
its hilt a silver cross—drawn forth now lets
hot radiant blood slide
from bubbling nostrils
through cloth to thirsty ground.

Yearning horns found
fleeing cloth and bloodless pillow,
substance none. Arrogant thighs,
that swiped and turned death by,
now, close as love, above lean lunging,
filling the pain-hot eye.

That stares till it turns to blood.
With the short knife dug
quick!
to the nape.
And the thick
neck drops on the spot of the cape.

Chains are drawn
round the horns, whose points are clean.
Trumpets shout.
New sand is thrown
where death's blood streamed.
Four stout,
jingling horses with gilded hooves
tug death out.

Life is awarded ears and flowers.
Pelted with hats and shoes, and praise,
glittering life, in tight pink thighs,
swaggers around a rotunda of screams and *Oles*.

Death is dragged from the ring,
a clumsy hide,
a finished thing—
back to his pen.
The gate swings shut.

The gate swings wide.
Here comes trotting, snorting death
let loose again.

INSTEAD OF THE CAMARGUE

1

We hoped to find wild bulls and flamingos.
There were none there.
At Fos-sur-Mer
the wind whittled the gray sea to shingles

that, slanting, ran the reeds down.
Foils well-tempered,
they flew up again. Wind whimpered
over the fissured ramparts of the town.

We climbed to explore its church.
With the stone head of an elf
for tower, it sat on a stone shelf
high-hinged above the sea. This windy porch

held, as well, an ancient cemetery.
Marble-gabled steep *maisons,*
snug against *toutes les saisons,*
each housed a reliquary.

Tall, windowless sheds of tiny
width, in narrow yards— We wondered, were
the rag-robed bones standing within, for
they could not be lying. Shiny

nickel hearts, wreaths of mineral
flowers, fat sugar-white crosses,
and ceramic brooches bearing verses,
hung behind the ornate fences. No funeral

atmosphere. More like carnival.
For instance, rumps of rosy angels
fringed a tinted image of *Cher Papa.* Spangled
silver lilies blanketed a doll-

faced, smiling child
asleep in an ormolu pavilion; he hugged
a pink lamb that looked like candy. Tugged
by the wind (that failed

to fade or kill them) wax tulips, pansies,
peonies profused out of fix-footed urns.
On gilded grapes and vines
cherubs climbed in delicate frenzies

of carver's art: an arbor
of iron fruit and iron shade
stood over a dead husband. Widow had built a harbor

durable as could be, for his soul's rest.
A populous white fondant and fuss of graves:
crosses shouldered each other, conclaves
of many identicals of the dying Christ

plastered on the chests
and foreheads of the huts—that stood for
bodies needing no roof and no floor—
a labyrinth, a jagged forest.

And where a flayed, white figurine
twined snakish on an occasional black
cross, or burned black on a gold one, the crack
in conformity frightened; the thin,

writhing form, sweating
in redundant chorused pain
against the dark grain,
was like a voodoo sign. Forgetting

to enter the *église*—outside
a Virgin with downcast eyes and upbent lips
held out the robust Child, her hand beneath His hips—
we wandered the macabre compound where He died

in every yard. And came to a miniature cathedral
with encrusted spires of colored tile,
even a little pointed window, playhouse style,
in the side, leaded and stained—a tetrahedral

tomb caked with carvings. On its gothic portal:
"Ici repose Maman aux bras de Dieu."

A tight embrace, we thought. And were it true,
her head must reach the belfry, she'd displace the altar.

At a neglected gate, two angels, kneeling,
clapped between broken
wings like violet mussel shells, raised stricken,
noseless faces to a peeling

shrine of metal, now corroded,
roofless. Beneath, a pair of marble beds,
moss-browned, sunk in weeds,
could not be read, the inscriptions faded.

But ovals of porcelain rimmed
with filigree forget-me-nots
and painted bleeding hearts,
their baked designs undimmed,

depended from the necks of the bitten
tombstones side by side.
We leaned to read
what graceful brush had written:

A Notre Fils   *A Notre Fille*

Il est passé   *Toi qui passa*
Comme un nuage   *Comme un nuage*
Comme un flot   *Emportant au Ciel*
Rapide en son cours   *Notre amour*
Et nos cœurs   *Nos cœurs garderont*
Gardent son image   *Ton image*
Toujours   *Toujours*

There were many "beds" most
neatly made, side by side and close together,
and unnumbered "houses" that the weather
would take long to unpost,

but the cracked stone
covers over these children (who had slept away
how many hundred birthdays in the clay?)
would soon be thrown

among the shards and slabs that leaned
in a corner of the wall—
the thick wall around this stone metropole,
that defended and screened

it from the living still at loose. We
moved bemused in its gravel alleys, peeping
into curious stalls of the fête the dead were keeping
open above the sea.

Past a mélange of flamboyant and somber things,
butterflies (of pressed paper), hectic flowers,
black-wrapped stars and harps, and wire
hourglasses with wings,

we came to the gate's gap, where the wind squalled
and sun smote the rock stair
going down. In a corner there,
by sharp dark cypress enwalled,

was hidden a tomb square and plain:
A lean and beautiful lion
couchant on the lid—rivet-eyed scion
and emblem of France—his mane

a cowl of grim, roughened stone
black from the rains. One paw was bent
on the lock of the grave, but negligent,
upturned, the other—as all lions are known

to lie—guardianship
alerting his nostrils, his chest raised.
His cool, secret smile grazed
us, and the ancient patience at his lip.

Chiseled below, on his pedestal:
*"Ici repose Le Gendarme Pierre
Pecot, Tué Par Un Braconnier,
1752"*—within a wreath of laurel.

We saw no wild bulls or flamingos that day.
To reach the Camargue, we agreed
we would need
to have gone by another way—

north, then west around the delta of the Rhône.
Descending to the flats, we drove the straight
road between sea and slate
marsh, where rice is grown.

We saw shorebirds wade
near the floating corks
of fishermen's nets. Not Moroccan storks
or Egyptian ibises, as the guidebook had said,

but ordinary checkered sanderlings, and a lone heron.
We turned back through the red hills, *terres rougeâtres,* where
above the Etang de Berre,
the incessant mistral blows—and came to an environ

of Van Gogh. Great umber faces
headdressed in flames—round
ruffed faces, Indian and profound,
on totem stalks thick as maces—

stared: a company of giant
sunflowers. Like eclipses of the sun,
their plate-heads, almost black, spun
within the yellow aureoles; only the pliant

broad leaves sagged on their spikes in the heat.
East of the divide,
nearing Aix, on the cooler side,
the tranquil valley fell away. Cut wheat

stood in blond hives on the slant
hills. We passed fields of smoky lavender, ditches
full of poppies flaring like lit matches
and young grapevines planted

in ruled brown earth. The road became a funnel: arching
sycamores, their pinto-spotted trunks tan
and gray, with painted white belts, ran
by the car, the low sun torching

through. Beyond the opening of that shade-
striped bower,
Cézanne's mountain, Saint-Victoire,
unfolded its blue knife-blade

on the sky. Against the rind
of evening, its acute shape
blunted, enlarging on the landscape.
We circled fruit and olive orchards, poplar-lined,

and watched how shadows massed
in the concaves of that head,
the impenetrable Pharoah-face that baffled
all the painters of Provence, until Cézanne in his last

attempt, defined it with simple
brush as tender vapor, a mirage:
*"Au lieu de se tasser, immense et sauvage,
elle respire et participe toute bleutée de l'air ample."*

3

We never found the blackfaced bulls
and rouge flamingos, except on
postcards . . . We bought one
showing three skulls,

a rosary, and a knapsack
that are among Cézanne's effects
in his studio at Aix,
and twirling the rack

with other tourists on Cours Mirabeau,
also bought views of the exotic Camargue—the small
gray horses in tall
grass, the high-horned, stubborn *taureaux*—

and of gypsies at Fos-sur-Mer.
"La Mediterranée a une couleur comme les maquereaux,"
said the back of a card, quoting Van Gogh,
who used to walk there

"sur la plage déserte." We sat
sipping coffee in the oasis
of Aix, the fountain's breath in our faces,
remembering that

a sign by the cemetery gate had said: "It is forbidden
to photograph the houses of the dead."
We could not buy our lion, spread
dark and lean upon a card. We're glad he's hidden.

FOUNTAINS OF AIX

Beards of water
some of them have.
Others are blowing whistles of water.
Faces astonished that constant water
jumps from their mouths.
Jaws of lions are snarling water
through green teeth over chins of moss.
Dolphins toss jets of water
from open snouts
to an upper theatre of water.
Children are riding swans and water.
coils from the S-shaped necks and spills
in flat foils from pincered bills.
A solemn curly headed bull
puts out a swollen tongue of water.
Cupids naked are making water
into a font that never is full.
A goddess is driving a chariot through water.
Her reins and whips are tight white water.
Bronze hooves of horses wrangle with water.
Marble faces half hidden in leaves.
Faces whose hair is leaves and grapes
of stone are peering from living leaves.
Faces with mossy lips unlocked
always uttering water.
Water
wearing their features blank,
their ears deaf, their eyes mad
or patient or blind or astonished at water
always uttered out of their mouths.

THE ALYSCAMPS AT ARLES

            The bodies
that covered the bones
                  died.
       Then the bones
                  died.
       Now the stones
that covered the bones
          are dying
                in the Alyscamps at Arles.

                The lizard darts
                between thick lips
    of the hollow–bodied
            stones.
                Under the broken lids
                the scorpion lives
                transfixed.

    A sculptor who forms
      by destroying form,
        and finds form
                beneath,
    has peeled the bodies
   and found the bones,
has dwindled the bones
                till they snapped
                in the coffin-beds
        of the stones.
                Now he crumbles
                the heavy limbs
        of the stones
    that have been dying
                for two thousand years
                in the Alyscamps at Arles.

           Soft bodies
              died
                soonest.
              Flesh
                was a colored dew wiped off.
              Bones
                were chalk to the sculptor,

                        but he has been rubbing
at these stones
                        for two thousand years.

                        See, they have faces
                        with mouths and sockets!
                        See, in the shadows
                        of the poplars
                        are great square skulls
                        with noseholes dark,
                        like caves.
                        There, where the lizard
                        spreads his saurean hand.

                        Moonlight
puts a **flesh**
                        around the recumbent ribs.
of the stones.
                        When the passion
                        of the nightingale begins,
                        the sculptor
                        seems to sleep.

ABOVE THE ARNO

My room in Florence was the color of air.
Blue the stippled wall I woke to,
the tile floor white except where
shadowed by the washstand and my high
bed. Barefoot I'd go to the window to look
at the Arno. I'd open the broad shutters like a book,
and see the same scene. But each day's sky,
or night, dyed it a different light.

The lizard river might be green, or turbid gray,
or yellowish like the stucco palazzi
on the opposite quay.
Boys would be angling with long, lank
poles, sitting on the butts of them, dangling
legs from the paved bank;
they wore handkerchiefs, the corners knotted,
for caps against the strong

sun, and had their dogs along;
the dogs, brown-and-white spotted,
had to lie quiet. But I never saw anything
jerk the lines of the yellow poles.
The boys smoked a lot, and lazed in the sun.
Smaller ones dove and swam in the slow, snaking Arno
right under the sign that read: PERICOLO!
DIVIETO DI BAGNARSI.

Over Ponte Trinita, fiacres would go,
or a donkey-driven cart, among the auto
and popping scooter traffic. Freckled, gray,
blinkered horses trotted the red-and-black
carriages in which the richer tourists rode.
(A donkey looks like a bunny under its load,
with its wigwag ears and sweet expression;
the workman-driver flicks

a string-whip like a gadfly over it.)
I'd hear hoof-clops and heel-clicks
among hustling wheels on the bridge, that curved
like a violin's neck across the Arno.

It had two statues at each end—
white, graceful, a little funny.
One, a woman, had lost her head, but strode
forward holding her basket of fruit just the same.

You could see Giotto's Tower in my "book" and
the gold ball on top of Brunelleschi's Dome
and the clock with one hand
on the campanile of the Palazzo Vecchio,
and a blue slice of the Appenines the color of my room.
One day I slept all afternoon—
it was August and very hot—and didn't wake
until late at night,

or rather, early morning.
My mind was fresh—all was silent.
I crossed the white tiles, barefoot,
and opened the book of the shutters
to faint stars, to a full Arno,
starlight fingering the ripples. Gondola-slim
above the bridge, a new moon held a dim
circle of charcoal between its points.

Bats played in the greenish air,
their wing-joints
soft as moths' against the bone-gray palazzi where
not a window was alight,
the doorways dark as sockets.
Each of the four statues so white
and still,
rose somnambulistic from its hill

of stone, above the dusky slide
of the river. On my side,
a muscular, round-poled
man—naked behind—hugged a drape
against him, looking cold.
His partner, fat,
in short toga and hat
made of fruit, leaned a hand on a Horn

of Plenty. On the opposite bank, in torn
sweeping robes, a Signora
bore sheaves of wheat along her arm.
And, striding beside her with stately charm
in her broken flounces, the Headless One
offered her wealthy basket, chin
up—though I had to imagine
chin, face, head, headdress, all.

Then a tall
tower began to tell F O U R,
and another with different timbre spelled it
a minute later. Another mentioned it for the third time
in harsh bronze and slow.
Still another, with delicate chime
countered and cantered it. By now the sky had turned
della Robbia blue, the Arno yellowed silver.

I stood between the covers of my "book" and heard
a donkey's particular heels,
like syllables of a clear, quick word,
echo over the Arno. Then came the scrape-clink
of milk cans lowered on cobbles. And with the moon still
there, but transparent, the sky began to fill
with downy clouds—pink
as the breasts of Botticelli's Venus—foretinting dawn.

A BOY LOOKING AT BIG DAVID

I'm touching his toe.
I know I'll be brave after this.
His toenail wide as my hand,
I have to stand tall to reach it.

The big loose hand with the rock in it
by his thigh
is high above my head. The vein
from wrist to thumb, a blue strain in the marble.

As if it had natural anatomy all its own
inside it.
Somebody skinned off the top stone,
and there He stands.

I'd like to climb up there on that slippery Hip,
shinny up to the Shoulder
the other side of that thumping Neck,
and lie in the ledge on the collar-bone,

by the sling.
In that cool place
I'd stare-worship that big, full-lipped,
frown-browned, far-eyed, I-dare-you-Face.

I'd like to live on that David for a while,
get to know
how to be immortal like Him.
But I can only reach his Toe—

broad, poking over the edge of the stand.
So cool . . .
Maybe, marble Him,
he likes the warm of my hand?

NOTES MADE IN THE PIAZZA SAN MARCO

The wingéd lion on top of that column
(his paws have been patched, he appears to wear boots)
is bronze but has a white eye—
his tail sails out long . . . Could it help him fly?

On the other column St. Theodore
standing on an alligator,
he and it as white as salt,
wears an iron halo and an iron sword.

San Marco is crusty and curly with many crowns,
or is it a growth of golden thrones?
The five domes
covered, it looks like, with stiff crinkly parachute silk

have gold balls on twigs on turnip-tips,
sharp turrets in between with metal flags that cannot wave.
On all their perches statues gay and grave:
Erect somewhere among the towers a tall-necked woman

wearing an of-course-gold coronet
is helping a beast with baboon's head and lion's body to stand
on hindlegs. She's placing her hand
in his mouth . . . I wonder why.

In recesses of arches half in shade
are robed Venetians made
of red, blue, gold, green mosaics small as caramels,
fishermen encumbered by their robes launching a boat,

their faces all pricked out with those square
skin-colored pores . . .
Above them in a gold sky angels fly standing up.
About to step off the balcony

in the center of the main façade, four
horses exactly as big as horses but consciously more
handsome—gold running in rivulets
from their shoulders to under their bellies, their necks'

curt blade-shaped manes sloping like Roman helmets—
have a pair of heads front
and a pair to the side,
the lips tugged back into wide

loops. The bits are absent.
A pink and white checkered palace relatively plain
with a pleasant loggia half way up
puts a rectangle out to the quay of the Grand Canal:

On one of its corners Adam and Eve look rueful, the Tree
between them—its low branches with leaves attached
happen to cover their genitals. Three
times hugged around the trunk, the serpent laughs.

There's often a rush of pigeons in the Piazza,
a leather scarf swept past your eyes
as if snatched from the ground,
when from the campanile great tongues let loose

and flog you, and flog you with gouts of iron sound.
The air must always burn deep blue here—
a velvet box for all that gold and white.
It turns thin and clear

toward the water. The Canal is a green vase lying down.
Gondolas knock their tethered necks on the quay:
Black, saddled with red, riderless, restless, they
are touching hips and shifting on the single-footing waves.

THE PANTHEON, ROME

Outside, pacing the sunken ramp around it
are many cats, scrofulous and starving.
The flutings of the columns of the portico
are bitten with age, their bases dark and urinous.
But the circle, the triangle, the square,
a solid geometric with caplike top,
squats here grimly eternal. Sixteen legs,
Corinthian, bear it up under the pronaos,
plain, harmonious. In gouges of the walls,
on accidental pediments of destroyed stone,
the fierce-eyed cats have taken occupation.

On a day of rain I pass into the interior,
through a door of bronze and leather—one slab
of which is agape. Inside is granite dusk
and dungeon cold—the round room no longer lined
with statues, the vault stripped of its gilt tiles.
Yet, there strike upon my chest the radii of grandeur.

The circle is large, the floor an immense coin
of porphyry and pavonazzetto; the dome of lead
is a strong belly; its rows of boxed blind windows
incise the entablature to the open disk at the top—
umbilical and only orifice for light.
That high lidless hole left for the sun to grin through
has not been closed since Agrippa.
Through it, now, rain rushes freely down
on the temple floor, to scour the dull colors
of the pattern that repeats, in giallo antico,
the eternal circle, the just square.

I walk around the tall, splattering column of rain
in the gloom. In a gray niche a dusty Christ
is stretched aloft—feet crossed and twisted,
head shadowed by iron thorns. On a shabby fresco
almost effaced, Mary with a stare of consternation
hears the Angel's smug pronouncement of her state.

Stooping, I discover Raphael's tomb, a bare stone box,
in a recess near the floor. Dust, thick as chalk,

powders the organ pipes, and the crude block
of the altar—installed when the Pantheon
was Christianized by Boniface in 609.
This temple stood before the Popes—
and Jove before Jesus—Minerva before the Virgin.
That empty arched embrasure remembers Bacchus laughing.
The rain that cannot ruin the floor,
the cats with demon eyes that crouch
around these walls, are fitting, and good.

ITALIAN SAMPLER

Lombardy, Tuscany, Umbria, Calabria.
A spear of leaves. A pear.
A clod-filled pasture dark as a bear.
Yellow blazes around a crown.

Lombardy, Tuscany, Umbria, Calabria.
Somber oxen. September flares.
Wind and silk, parchment and candles.
Slumberous, plushy, ponderous, elaborate.

A tree, a fruit, a pigment, an ornament.
Plumes, juices, bristles, crystals.
A mast. A horn. A bramble. A bride.
Lombardy, Tuscany, Umbria, Calabria.

WHILE SITTING IN THE TUILERIES AND FACING
THE SLANTING SUN

There is the Line
There is the Circle
the bending Line
the expanding Circle
There is the moving Line
but the still Circle
but the enlarging Circle
the lengthening Line

The Crack
and the Particle
the deepening Crack
the doubling redoubling Particle
the Splitting
and Resplitting
then the Multiple
the opening Closing
then the closure Opening

There is a Swaddled Thing
There is a Swaddled Thing
There is a Rocking Box
There is a Covered Box

The Unwrapping
the Ripening
Then the Loosening
the Spoiling
The Stiffening
then the Wrapping
The Softening
but the long long Drying

The Wrapping
the Wrapping
the Straightening

and Wrapping
The rigid Rolling
the gilded Scrolling
The Wrapping
and Wrapping
and careful Rewrapping
The Thinning
and Drying
but the Wrapping
and Fattening

There is the worm Coiled
and the straw Straightened
There is the Plank
and the glaucous Bundle
the paper Skull
and the charred Hair
the linen Lip
and the leather Eyelid

There is a Person
of flesh that is *a rocking* *Box*
There is a Box
of wood that is *a painted* *Person*

NOTE FROM A DIARY: I sat an hour on a bench in the Tuileries
by a frozen flower bed. The sunrays striking between my lashes
made gilt slits, black dots. I felt rolled up in a spool of
light—face warm, feet numb—a kind of mesmerization . . .
And remembered Giotto's fresco, "Birth of the Virgin" in a
cloister in Florence: the "Mother of God" was a swaddled infant
held upright, like a board or plaque, by her nurse—the halo
a gilt bonnet around the tiny head with its fugitive eyes . . .
And I remembered a mummy in the Vatican Museum in Rome: in her
sarcophagus shaped and painted like herself, an Egyptian girl
2000 years old lay unwrapped to the waist, and with hands and
feet bare—her nails, hair, lips and eyelids frangible as tobacco
leaf, but intact. Still exquisite, merely dried and darkened,
was her youth.

42

A HURRICANE AT SEA

Slowly a floor rises, almost becomes a wall.
Gently a ceiling slips down, nearly becomes a floor.
A floor with spots that stretch, as on a breathing
animal's hide. It rises again with a soft lurch.

The floor tilts, is curved, appears to be racing north
with a pattern of dents and dips
over slashes of dark. Now there are white lips,
widening on the wall

that stands up suddenly. The ceiling is all
rumpled, snarled, as a wet animal's fur.
The floor hardens, humps up like rock,
the side of a hill too slant to walk.

White teeth are bared where lazy lips swam.
The ceiling is the lid of a box about to slam.
Is this a real floor I walk? It's an angry spine
that shoots up over a chasm of seething

milk—cold, churned, shoving the stern around.
There's the groaning sound
of a cauldron about to buckle, maybe break.
A blizzard of glass and lace

shivers over this dodging box.
It glides up the next high hissing alp—halts
on top. But the top turns hollow while the hollow spins.
I run down a slope and feel like twins,

one leg northeast, one west.
The planks pitch leeward, level an instant, then
rear back to a flat, stunned rest.
It's frightening, that vacant moment. I feel

the Floor beneath the floor reel,
while a thickening wilderness is shunted aft, under.
I'm in a bottle becalmed, but a mountain bloats
ahead, ready to thunder

on it. The floor is rushed into the pit.
Maybe there's no bottom to it.
I'm burried in a quarry, locked in a bucking
room—or bottle, or box—near cracking,

that's knocked about in a black,
enormous, heavy, quaking Room.
Is there a bottom to it? I'm glad not to have to know.
Boulders, canyon-high, smash down on the prow,

are shattered to snow, and shouldered off somehow.
Tossed out again on top. Topside bounced
like a top, to scoot the bumpy floor . . .
Out there, it's slicked to a plane almost, already,

though chopped with white to the far baseboard.
The ceiling is placing
itself right, getting steadier,
licking itself smooth. The keel

takes the next swollen hills along their backs—
like a little dog gripped
to a galloping horse—slipping
once in a while, but staying on.

TO MIX WITH TIME 3

···cubes and cones···

SNOW IN NEW YORK

It snowed in New York. I walked on Fifth
Avenue and saw the orange snowplow cut the drifts
with rotary sickles, suck up celestial clods into its turning neck,
a big flue that spewed them into a garbage truck.
This gift from the alps was good for nothing, though scarcely gray.
The bright apparatus, with hungry noise,
crumbled and mauled the new hills. Convoys
of dump-cars hauled them away.

I went to Riker's to blow my nose
in a napkin and drink coffee for its steam. Two rows
of belts came and went from the kitchen, modeling scrambled
eggs, corn muffins, bleeding triangles of pie.
Tubs of dirty dishes slid by.
Outside the fogged window black bulking people stumbled
cursing the good-for-nothing whiteness. I thought
of Rilke, having read how he wrote

to Princess Marie von Thurn und Taxis, saying: "The idea haunts
    me—
it keeps on calling—I must make a poem for Nijinski
that could be, so to say, swallowed and then danced." Printed
as on the page, in its
remembered place in the paragraph, that odd name with three dots
over the *iji*, appeared—as I squinted
through the moist window past the traveling
dishes—against the snow. There unraveled

from a file in my mind a magic notion
I, too, used to play with: from chosen words a potion
could be wrung; pickings of them, eaten, could make you fly, walk
on water, be somebody else, do or undo anything, go back
or forward on belts of time. But then I thought:
Snow in New York is like poetry, or clothes made of roses.
Who needs it, what can you build with snow, who can you feed?
    Hoses
were coming to whip back to water, wash to the sewers the nuisance-
    freight.

FROM THE OFFICE WINDOW

My attention the frame for
a complication of city roofs:
Various levels, shapes,
perspectives, angles. Puffs

from chimneys, ruffled flags
on a school tower. Ectomorphic
shadows, flats of late light.
Distant pigeons diving, cloud surf

slow-unrolling. A red
construction crane north-leaning,
then south. Scrawl of a jet
half-circling, caning

the sky. A monster of many surfaces
rises to the split-second net
of my eye. How to beach it?
Strokes of a pen, fleet

washes of a brush would
fetch it eventually almost exact.
The process would be tedious,
the body stiff, unlit

at capture. A camera might
harpoon, arrest
the big thing whole—but gray
and small. A cinema projector

would gulp and then expel
it life-sized, intact in all
details, the entire whale
still swimming. But the soul

would be hooked, and have to repeat
itself just like that:
Chimneys never
ceasing their white

evacuations. Shadows
never slipping.
Flicking flags
forever flicking.

Pigeons always slanting
at that distance. The brick whale
never darkening. *Its many scales
are already lamplit,*

the spouts and towers dark.
Words? Let their
mutations work
toward the escape

of objects into the nearest next
shape, motion, assembly,
temporal context;
let the progeny of interlapping

shadows multiply . . .
*Façades of light!
Another cumbrous monster
has risen to my eye.*

AT THE MUSEUM OF MODERN ART

At the Museum of Modern Art you can sit in the lobby
on the foam-rubber couch; you can rest and smoke,
and view whatever the revolving doors express.
You don't have to go into the galleries at all.

In this arena the exhibits are free and have all
the surprises of art—besides something extra:
sensory restlessness, the play of alternation,
expectation in an incessant spray

thrown from heads, hands, the tendons of ankles.
The shifts and strollings of feet
engender compositions on the shining tiles,
and glide together and pose gambits,

gestures of design, that scatter, rearrange,
trickle into lines, and turn clicking through a wicket
into rooms where caged colors blotch the walls.
You don't have to go to the movie downstairs

to sit on red plush in the snow and fog
of old-fashioned silence. You can see contemporary
Garbos and Chaplins go by right here.
And there's a mesmeric experimental film

constantly reflected on the flat side of the wide
steel-plate pillar opposite the crenellated window.
Non-objective taxis surging west, on Fifty-third,
liquefy in slippery yellows, dusky crimsons,

pearly mauves—an accelerated sunset, a roiled
surf, or cloud-curls undulating—their tubular ribbons
elongations of the coils of light itself
(engine of color) and motion (motor of form.)

A FIXTURE

Women women women women
in a department store
with hats on (hats in *it*)
and shoes on (shoes in *it*)
dresses coats gloves on (and *in*
all the departments)

In the lobby (in a niche)
between two glass revolving doors
sluff sluff sluff sluff
(rubber bottoms of whirling doors)
flick flick click click
(women in women out) sits a nun

In the mid-whirl (a station)
white black wooden (a fixture)
holding a wooden cup she sits
between the glitter of double doors
hexagonal glasses glittering
over glassy fixed eyes

A garter snake of black
beads (wooden?) catching light
crawling (clicking) crawling
(clicking) up her draped
fixed short carved
black knees (thighs)

Her white hat (hood) a head cover
her shoes short black
flat (foot covers)
her dress a black curtain (cape)
over a longer curtain shape
she is the best dressed

RIDING THE "A"

I ride
the "A" train
and feel
like a ball-
bearing in a roller skate.
I have on a gray
rain-
coat. The hollow
of the car
is gray.
My face
a negative in the slate
window,
I sit
in a lit
corridor that races
through a dark
one. Strok-
ing steel,
what a smooth rasp—it feels
like the newest of knives
slicing
along
a long
black crusty loaf
from West 4th to 168th.
Wheels
and rails
in their prime
collide,
make love in a glide
of slickness
and friction.
It is an elation
I wish to pro-
long.
The station
is reached
too soon.

New York

PIGEON WOMAN

Slate, or dirty-marble-colored,
or rusty-iron-colored, the pigeons
on the flagstones in front of the
Public Library make a sharp lake

into which the pigeon woman wades
at exactly 1:30. She wears a
plastic pink raincoat with a round
collar (looking like a little

girl, so gay) and flat gym shoes,
her hair square-cut, orange.
Wide-apart feet carefully enter
the spinning, crooning waves

(as if she'd just learned how
to walk, each step conscious,
an accomplishment); blue knots in the
calves of her bare legs (uglied marble),

age in angled cords of jaw
and neck, her pimento-colored hair,
hanging in thin tassles, is gray
around a balding crown.

The day-old bread drops down
from her veined hand dipping out
of a paper sack. Choppy, shadowy ripples,
the pigeons strike around her legs.

Sack empty, she squats and seems to rinse
her hands in them—the rainy greens and
oily purples of their necks. Almost
they let her wet her thirsty fingertips—

but drain away in an untouchable tide.
A make-believe trade
she has come to, in her lostness
or illness or age—to treat the motley

city pigeons at 1:30 every day, in all
weathers. It is for them she colors
her own feathers. Ruddy-footed
on the lime-stained paving,

purling to meet her when she comes,
they are a lake of love. Retreating
from her hands as soon as empty,
they are the flints of love.

CAT & THE WEATHER

Cat takes a look at the weather:
snow;
puts a paw on the sill;
his perch is piled, is a pillow.

Shape of his pad appears:
will it dig? No,
not like sand,
like his fur almost.

But licked, not liked:
too cold.
Insects are flying, fainting down.
He'll try

to bat one against the pane.
They have no body and no buzz,
and now his feet are wet;
it's a puzzle.

Shakes each leg,
then shakes his skin
to get the white flies off;
looks for his tail,

tells it to come on in
by the radiator.
World's turned queer
somehow: all white,

no smell. Well, here
inside it's still familiar.
He'll go to sleep until
it puts itself right.

1

A cannon's mouth. A
clock. The heads of
two gargoyles on a
butcher's block. No blood,
however. Blue and green
opaque panels pretend to
be   air.

2

If a window were there,
we'd breathe pebbles.
The night tastes burrs
in the full moon's hair.

3

A
queen
has
just
    passed
by
for
the
spore
of
her
    train
    is
        seen
            on
        the
        floor.

4

This
yellow
rectangle
might be light
except it's thick;
you could stir
it with a
stick
had
you
come
sooner.

5

Sir: High up on a trestle created by your eyelashes
when you blink, a very tiny train, the   kind   that
chugs,
and a

                                white
                                scald
                                above
                                 its
                                bald
                                head,
is moving, making you think several black bugs   bump
                            softly.

                    6

Several black bugs bump softly.
Several
          black
                bugs
                      bump
                            softly.

                                            7

                                Yes, elephant
                                gray   is
                                d o m i n a n t .

                8

Although these arches d w i n d l e
alarmingly, there's no harm. Try the
doorknobs; the sea won't leak through.

                            9

                        The foreground's reassuring--
                        it slants backward.
                                        That
                                    shadow
                                     is
                                     a
                                    hill
                        of flowing sand.
                        Slick in places.
        10   Take my hand.   Ah, here's the
                            escalator
        Kick   leading
        Kick   down
        Kick   to
        Kick   sleep.
        Kick
        Kick
        Kick

Kick
Kick
these
eggs
out
of
the
way
without breaking any.
Not difficult—they're
flat—only pasted on;
they can't roll, for
the tiles are rose.
But the toes of our
boots must be reno-
vated accordingly.

11

One more trapezoid left to be
crossed—the sole piece of
furniture on the lower
level. A stern jerk at
the bit will do it . . .
There might be a
rubber mitten
nailed beside
the brow of a
Greek in
plaster,
b u t
don't
stop
for
that
now.

12

Gallop around the kid body of a doll. With stitches prominent from crotch to navel.

The double gleam of needles lifts the horizon to stilts. Then the path, or slab, or wall wilts. We flounder in melted cheese or candle-droppings.

13

Stop! Notice that the ground is S K Y solidified.

14

Let us recall that the infinite number resembles the Figure 6, reflected in any smooth convex surface well-buffed. The frame is only lumber. Let us e-merge. E-merge on the threshold of the unexpected, where all rays, all rays, all rays employed here, converge.

SOUTHBOUND ON THE FREEWAY

A tourist came in from Orbitville,
parked in the air, and said:

The creatures of this star
are made of metal and glass.

Through the transparent parts
you can see their guts.

Their feet are round and roll
on diagrams—or long

measuring tapes—dark
with white lines.

They have four eyes.
The two in the back are red.

Sometimes you can see a 5-eyed
one, with a red eye turning

on the top of his head.
He must be special—

the others respect him,
and go slow,

when he passes, winding
among them from behind.

They all hiss as they glide,
like inches, down the marked

tapes. Those soft shapes,
shadowy inside

the hard bodies—are they
their guts or their brains?

WHEN YOU LIE DOWN, THE SEA STANDS UP

Thick twisted cables
                of bottle glass at the base,
gunbarrel-blue higher up,
  are quickly being braided and stretched,
their condition molten,
                                their surface cold.
Or they are the long smooth logs of a pile
                being built from the top down.
The trunks of greatest girth
                arrive at the bottom
with silver rips and ridges in their bark.

                There is a wall in motion
like a lathe of light
                and dark galvanic blue
layers which are twirling,
                extending beyond your eye-points.
You cannot see their ends.

                Watch the topmost thinnest strand,
too taut to quiver:
                Above is a calcimined ceiling,
heliotrope . . . steady . . .
                delicate as for a bedroom.

THE CONTRAPTION

Going up is pleasant. It tips your chin,
and you feel tall and free
as if in control of, and standing in
a chariot, hands feeling the frisky

reins. But, doubled in your seat,
knuckled to the fun-car's handrails,
you mount baby-buggied, cleat by cleat,
to that humped apogee your entrails

aren't ready for. Wind in your
ears, clouds in your eyes, it's easy
to define the prophetic jelly at your core
as joy. The landscape of amusement goes queasy

only when the gilded buckboard juts straight out
over undippered air. A jaw of horror will spill
you? Not yet. The route
becomes a roaring trough for the next hill

hairpinning higher. You wish you had
the chance to count how many ups,
downs and switchbacks the mad
rattler, rearing its steel hoops, has. The divan hiccups

over a straightaway now, at mild speed.
Then you look: Jolly carousel and ferris wheel, far
years beneath, are cruel gears you can be emptied
into over the side of the hellish sled. Star-

beaded sky! (It feels better to look higher.) How
did the morning, the whole blue-and-white day
go by in what seems one swoop? You vow
to examine the contraption and its fairway,

measure the system of gruesome twists,
the queer dimensions, if ever you get down. Going
down is a dull road. Your fists
loosen, pretend no longer, knowing

they grip no stick of purpose. The final chutes are
unspectacular, slower repetitious of past
excitements. A used and vulgar car
shovels you home in a puzzling gloom. The vast

agitation faded in your bowels, you think
that from the ground you'll trace the rim
your coaster sped and crawled, the sink
and rise, the reason for its shape. Grim

darkness now. The ride
is complete. You are positioned for discovery, but,
your senses gone, you can't see the upper arching works. Wide
silence. Midnight. The carnival is shut.

TRINITY CHURCHYARD, SPRING 1961

Thin shoulders of the old stones,
rude weathered signals of the dead,
armless and as if wearing square
robes, some with an outcrop rounded

as the head once was. Some dark
and marred as charcoal, slices broken,
are torsos rugged earth holds steady here,
perpetual in rain and wind and under

the shrill file of the years.
Some that were white have yellowed
in the sun, bent back in a stasis,
tipped by time, as candles lopped

or shortened with their use. The names
have run awry as melted wax.
Their burning has been opposite to green
and flame-shaped buds exploding now.

Gaunt remnants of one great skeleton
awaiting assembly by the church's side,
(she herself a saintly corpse
hidden in a corner of the town,

a soot-cowled ornament among the tall,
smooth-sided tombs of glass
whose ostentatious signals on the sky
heedless ask their own erasure)

their shadows grow and, longer than themselves,
repeat them on their owned and ancient grass.
Among the dead-to-be, that multiply,
huddle the frail dead undestroyed.

THE TOTEM

We live in the
radius of this
tower. Cocked
at heaven, its
pike is visible
from every quarter.
At night, sabers of
light from its tip
encompass two rivers.
Every forty seconds
the wide shears separate;
raised arms in bishop's
robes impose a mechanical
blessing on all roofs.
By day, the arrogant flint-gray
stock—square, printed with
windows—takes aim at the sun.
Or else, ethereal, decapitated by
fog, it sits, a pale alp
on false distance. From high in
the sides of lesser towers, its
naked neck and shoulders of an obese
bottle occupies the frame of every
window. On any corner—north, south,
east, west—a lift of the head finds
the totem-shape, the boss-god's profile
regnant, its four faces caressed by cloud,
granite, ever the same.
From the apex of
this tower, on a parapet, our bodies boxed by
the wind, we feel the tremor of the heavy stake
screwed into the engine of the city. It quivers
as if transmitting the rub of our planet's axiel
twist. Here we scan our compact kingdom: a geometrized
platform, one wedge in the sea, loaded with cubes
and cones, a chaos of knives flashing upright to the
south. In the north, straight-edged blocks and rulers,
within which, quaintly, a yard—a quadrangle of actual
earth—retains the nap of trees and grass. To east and
west, curving skeins of rails and highways, bridges webbing
the rivers; serene, arrowed with craft, they hug our island's
sides. Straight down a hundred floors, in fissures and
crossing furrows, diagonals of shadow and dusty light,
vehicles stitch the redundant maze. A human rug moves,
mottling the pavements. Foreshortened, we pour around our
totem's pedestal, and we pour in and out of its broad, hollow core.

We live in the radius of this tower. It is the hub of our
flat wheel of days. The semaphore at the ends of all our
avenues. Its head a vector, the terminal of our groundling
sight. Landmark and seamark. Sky-peg in the pilot's eye
as he glides down tilting floors of air. Moon and sun are midgeted
by its radiant, constant shaft. Its real sides we lean against—
neighbor and titan—stone, obedient glass and concrete
that is our home. Secure in the shadow—dense, pyramidal
dipped over the city that dyes us—we are content to be tiny—
proud in the beacons that bless us with a god's bayonet gaze.

64

DISTANCE AND A CERTAIN LIGHT

Distance
and a certain light
makes anything artistic—
it doesn't matter what.

From an airplane, all
that rigid splatter of the Bronx
becomes organic, logical
as web or beehive. Chunks

of decayed cars in junkyards,
garbage scows (nimble roaches
on the Harlem), herds of stalled
manure-yellow boxes on twisting reaches

of rails, are punched clean and sharp
as ingots in the ignition of the sun.
Rubbish becomes engaging shape—
you only have to get a bead on it,

the right light filling the corridor
of your view—a gob of spit
under a microscope, fastidious
in structure as a crystal. No contortion

without intention, and nothing ugly.
In any random, sprawling, decomposing thing
is the charming string
of its history—and what it will be next.

TO MIX WITH TIME 4

···colors take bodies···

THE SNOW GEESE AT JAMAICA BAY

A great wedge of snow geese wafted over,
their wings whiter than the white air,
thinned to a long line at one hypotenuse,
as the caravan turned, and pointed north,

a needle their leader, trailing two wavering
threads. Each pair of wings powerful and large,
but in the air, high, weightless as fleece
or petals blown, to lift within the pattern.

Arrowed, yet curved, their course unveering,
varying but carried forward in a ventral glide,
all the star-sharp forms taking their own tilt,
undulant crests on a proud swell, heaving,

hoisting its feather-body toward a divined coast.
And a blue goose flew with them in the dwindling
end of their line. Cooler his color
than the buttermilk breasts of the others,

his dark feet stretched out, his wings
of evening snow. A strange and related other,
denser chip let go, to weight a pure design,
in the wild wedge melted last into the sky.

LIVING TENDERLY

My body a rounded stone
with a pattern of smooth seams.
My head a short snake,
retractive, projective.
My legs come out of their sleeves
or shrink within,
and so does my chin.
My eyelids are quick clamps.

My back is my roof.
I am always at home.
I travel where my house walks.
It is a smooth stone.
It floats within the lake,
or rests in the dust.
My flesh lives tenderly
inside its bone.

THE WOODS AT NIGHT

The binocular owl,
fastened to a limb
like a lantern
all night long,

sees where all
the other birds sleep:
towhee under leaves,
titmouse deep

in a twighouse,
sapsucker gripped
to a knothole lip,
redwing in the reeds,

swallow in the willow,
flicker in the oak—
but cannot see
whip-poor-will

under the hill
in deadbrush nest,
who's awake, too—
with stricken eye

flayed by the moon
her brindled breast
repeats, repeats, repeats its plea
for cruelty.

ANOTHER SPRING UNCOVERED

Colors take bodies,
become many birds.
Odors are born
as earliest buds.
Sounds are streams,
the pebbles bells.
Embraces are
the winds and woods.

Hills of lambskin
stroke our feet.
We move in an amnion
of light,
fondle moss
and put our cheeks
to birches
and warm slate

sides of rocks.
Cardinal on a limb
gripped: if we
could take him
into our hand,
the whistling red
feather-pulse,
the velvet plum—

and seize those other
hues, hot, cool:
indigo bunting sky-piece,
olive thrush
in brown shadow,
oriole apricot-breasted,
hush-wing harlequin
towhee—alive!

If we could eat snowdrops,
sip hyacinths,

make butterflies
be bows in our hair,
wade the tinkling streams
of innocence,
wear lambskin grass,
and suck but milk of air!

ONE MORNING IN NEW HAMPSHIRE

We go to gather berries of rain
(sharp to the eye as ripe to the tongue)
that cluster the woods and, low down
between rough-furrowed pine
trunks, melons of sunlight. Morning, young,
carries a harvest in its horn:
colors, shapes, odors, tones
(various as senses are keen).
High in a grape-transparent fan
of boughs are cones
of crystal that were wooden brown.

Two by two, into our ears
are fed sweet pips from a phoebe's throat,
and buzzy notes from a warbler pair,
nuts chuckled from the score
of the thrasher. Gauzing afloat,
a giant moth comes to the choir,
and hums while he sips
from spangles of fern. Insects whir
like wheat in a circular
bin of light; we hear skip
the husking chipmunks in their lair.

Goblin pears, or apples, or quaint
eggs, the mushrooms
litter the forest loft
on pungent mats, in shade still wet,
the gray of gunny in the gloom—
in sun, bright sawdust.
Here's a crop for the nose:
(relish to sight as motley to scent):
fume of cobwebbed stumps, musky roots,
resin-tincture, bark-balm, dayspring moss
in stars new-pricked (vivid as soft).

Day heats and mellows. Those winking seeds—
or berries—spill from their pods; the path's dry

from noon wood to meadow. A speckled
butterfly on top of a weed is a red
and yellow bloom: if that two-ply
petal could be touched,
or the violet wing of the mountain!
Both out of reach—too wary,
or too far to stroke, unless with the eye.
But in green silk of the rye
grain our whole bodies are cuddled.

In the sun's heart we are ripe
as fruits ourselves, enjoyed
by lips of wind our burnished slopes.
All round us dark, rapt
bumble-eyes of susans are deployed
as if to suck our honey-hides. Ants nip,
tasting us all over
with tickling pincers. We are a landscape
to daddy-long-legs, whose ovoid
hub on stilts climbs us like a lover,
trying our dazzle, our warm sap.

A COUPLE

A bee
rolls
in the yellow
rose.
Does she
invite his hairy
rub?
He scrubs
himself
in her creamy
folds.
A bullet soft imposes
her spiral and, spinning, burrows
to her dewy
shadows.
The gold
grooves almost
match
the yellow
bowl.
Does his touch
please
or scratch?
When he's
done
his honey-
thieving
at her matrix,
whirs free
leaving,
she
closes,
still
tall, chill,
unrumpled on her stem.

JAPANESE BREAKFAST

The table of the pool is set.
Each cup quivers by a plate.

Some are filled with tea of sun,
some have pinks of liquor in;

some, thick and white, look upside down
as if put out to dry,

or not to use till morning
pours a thinner cream.

Lying out lopsided,
all the plates are green.

Immaculate as in Japan
the food is only dew,

but fountain-flounce, the table cloth,
shows a rainbow stain.

Some black-nosed goldfish passing through
on their way to shade

nudge the rocking saucers.
A wet ceramic toad,

descending stairs of moss
to breakfast on an insect,

upsets the level table top
but leaves the cups intact.

SEEING THE FROG

Seeing the frog
and on its back
embroidery like eyes,
I felt it "see" me
also as shadow
in disguise.

Lengthening
without motion
carefully my hand
lowered a socket—
and unclosed a pond.

Memory handed me
a frog,
pulse under thumb:
how to hold
a loose thing tight,
yet not lame.

The jerk, the
narrow hips' escape
happened again.
I felt the chill
embossment and
the ticking chin.

Before the splash
a hand spread
in whole design,
tan and shadow-
patched, the warts
of water mine!

FIREFLIES

Fireflies throw
love winks
to their kind
on the dark, glow
without heat,
their day bodies
common beetles.
In a planetarium
of the mind
sparks lit
when logic has gone
down
faint in the dawn
of intellect.
Instinct
makes luminous
the insect.
Idea's anonymous
ordinary mark,
that cryptic
in daylight crept,
can rise an asterisk
astonishing others out.
If the secret
of the dark
be kept,
an eagerness
in smallest, fiercest
hints
can scintillate.

THE CROSSING

With stealthy wing
the hawk crossed over
the air I breathed
and sank in some cover.

Through water I drank
the deer stepped slow
without chinking a stone
and slid into shadow.

The mountain's body ahead,
the same ground
I walked, hurried up
and out, away, and around

to where the distance stood.
It could not flee or hide.
I filled it. It filled me
and was satisfied.

THE EXCHANGE

Now my body flat,
the ground breathes,
I'll be the grass.

Populous and mixed is mind.
Earth take thought,
my mouth be moss.

Field go walking,
I a disk
will look down with seeming eye,

I will be time
and study to be evening.
You world, be clock.

I will stand,
a tree here,
never to know another spot.

Wind be motion,
birds be passion,
water invite me to your bed.

A CAGE OF SPINES 1

TABLE OF SPINES

ALMANAC

The hammer struck my nail, instead of nail.
A moon flinched into being. Omen-black,
it began its trail. Risen from horizon
on my thumb (no longer numb and indigo)
it waxed yellow, waned to a sliver that now
sets white, here at the rim I cut tonight.

I make it disappear, but mark its voyage
over my little oval ceiling that again
is cloudless, pink and clear. In the dark
quarter-inch of this moon before it arrived
at my nail's tip, an unmanned airship
dived 200 miles to the hem of space, and
vanished. At the place of Pharaoh Cheops'
tomb (my full moon floating yellow)
a boat for ferrying souls to the sun
was disclosed in a room sealed 5000 years.

Reaching whiteness, this moon-speck waned
while an April rained. Across the street,
a vine crept over brick up 14 feet. And
Einstein (who said there is no hitching
post in the universe) at 77 turned ghost.

THE CENTAUR

The summer that I was ten—
Can it be there was only one
summer that I was ten? It must

have been a long one then—
each day I'd go out to choose
a fresh horse from my stable

which was a willow grove
down by the old canal.
I'd go on my two bare feet.

But when, with my brother's jack-knife,
I had cut me a long limber horse
with a good thick knob for a head,

and peeled him slick and clean
except a few leaves for the tail,
and cinched my brother's belt

around his head for a rein,
I'd straddle and canter him fast
up the grass bank to the path,

trot along in the lovely dust
that talcumed over his hoofs,
hiding my toes, and turning

his feet to swift half-moons.
The willow knob with the strap
jouncing between my thighs

was the pommel and yet the poll
of my nickering pony's head.
My head and my neck were mine,

yet they were shaped like a horse.
My hair flopped to the side
like the mane of a horse in the wind.

My forelock swung in my eyes,
my neck arched and I snorted.
I shied and skittered and reared,

stopped and raised my knees,
pawed at the ground and quivered.
My teeth bared as we wheeled

and swished through the dust again.
I was the horse and the rider,
and the leather I slapped to his rump

spanked my own behind.
Doubled, my two hoofs beat
a gallop along the bank,

the wind twanged in my mane,
my mouth squared to the bit.
And yet I sat on my steed

quiet, negligent riding,
my toes standing the stirrups,
my thighs hugging his ribs.

At a walk we drew up to the porch.
I tethered him to a paling.
Dismounting, I smoothed my skirt

and entered the dusky hall.
My feet on the clean linoleum
left ghostly toes in the hall.

Where have you been? said my mother.
Been riding, I said from the sink,
and filled me a glass of water.

What's that in your pocket? she said.
Just my knife. It weighted my pocket
and stretched my dress awry.

Go tie back your hair, said my mother,
and *Why is your mouth all green?*
*Rob Roy, he pulled some clover
as we crossed the field,* I told her.

THE RED BIRD TAPESTRY

Now I put on the thimble of dream
   to stitch among leaves the red node of his body
and fasten here the few beads of his song.

Of the tree a cage of gilded spines
   to palace his scarlet, cathedral his cry,
and a ripple from his beak, I sew,
   a banner bearing seven studs,
this scarf to be the morning that received his stain.

I do with thought instead of actuality
   for it has flown.
With glinting thimble I pull back, pull back
   that freak of scarlet to his throne:

To worship him, enchanted cherry to a tree
   that never bore such fruit—
who tore the veil of possibility
   and swung here for a day,
a never-colored bird, a never-music heard,
   who, doubly wanded then, looped away.

To find, in hollow of my throat, his call,
   and try his note on all the flutes of memory,
until that clear jet rinses me
   that was his single play—
for this I wear his daring and his royal eye.

Now perfected, arrested in absence—
   my needle laid by and spread my hand—
his claws on stems of my fingers fastened,
   rooted my feet and green my brow,
I drink from his beak the seven beads dropping:
   I am the cage that flatters him now.

A LAKE SCENE

So innocent this scene, I feel I see it
   with a deer's eye,
uncovering a first secret from this shore.
   I think of the smoothest thing:
the inside of a young thigh,
   or the line of a torso when, supine,
the pectoral sheathe crosses the armpit
   to the outflung arm;
at the juncture of lake and hills, that zone,
   the lowest hill in weavings
of fainter others overlaid,
   is a pelvis in shadow.

The hazel waves slip toward me,
   the far arcade
honed by the sunset; nothing tears
   the transparent skin that water
and sky and, between them,
   the undulant horizon wears.
No contest here, no roughness,
   no threat,
the wind's lick mild as the lake's,
   the rock I lean on, moss-round
as that silhouette
   in the thwart of the opposite shore;
spruce and fir snug-wool its folds.

   My eye goes there, to the source
of a first secret. I would be inheritor
   of the lamb's way and the deer's,
my thrust take from the ground
   I tread or lie on. In thighs of trees,
in recumbent stones, in the loins
   of beasts is found
that line my own nakedness carried.
   Here, in an Eden of the mind,
I would remain among my kind,
   to lake and hill, to tree and beast married.

THE PROMONTORY MOMENT

Think of only now, and how this pencil
tilted in the sand, might be a mast,
its shadow to an ant marking the sun's place;
little and vast are the same to that big eye
that sees no shadow.

Think how future and past, afloat on an ocean
of breath, linked as one island,
might coexist with the promontory moment
around the sun's disc—for that wide eye
knows no distance or divide.

Over your shoulder in the circular cove, the sea,
woven by swimmers' gaudy heads, pulses an indigo
wing that pales at its frothy edge;
and, far out, sails as slow as clouds
change bodies as they come about.

Look at the standing gull, his pincered beak
yellow as this pencil, a scarlet streak beneath the tip,
the puff of his chest bowl-round and white,
his cuff-button eye of ice and jet
fixed on the slicing waves; shingle-snug, his gray wing
tucked to his side. Aloft, that plumpness,
whittled flat, sits like a kite.

Turn to where fishermen rise from a neck
of rock, rooted and still, rods played like spouts
from their hips, until, beneath the chips of waves,
a cheek rips on the barb, a silver soul is flipped
from the sea's cool home into fatal air.

Close your eyes and hear the toss of the waves'
innumerable curls on the brow of the world—
that head is shaggy as Samson's, and three-fourths
furred. And *now* is eternal in beard and tress
piled green, blown white on churned sand,
the brand of the past an ephemeral smutch
of brown seaweed cast back to the sucking surf.

Tomorrow the marge is replaced
by a lace of shells, to be gathered again
by the hairy sea when it swells; here nothing is built
or grown, and nothing destroyed; and the buoyed
mind dares to enmirror itself,
as the prone body, bared to the sun,
is undone of its cares.

The eye, also a sun, wanders,
and all that it sees it owns;
the filled sail, tacking the line between water
and sky, its mast as high as this pencil,
becomes the gull's dropped quill, and the fleece
of the wave, and the sea robin's arc
now stilled on the rock.

FOUNTAIN PIECE

A bird
is perched
upon a wing

The wing
is stone
The bird
is real

A drapery
falls about this form
The form is stone
The dress is rain

The pigeon preens his own
and does not know
he sits upon a wing
The angel does not feel
a relative among her large
feathers stretch
and take his span
in charge
and leave her there
with her cold
wings that cannot fold
while his fan
in air.

The fountain raining
wets the stone
but does not know it dresses
an angel in its tresses

Her stone cheek smiles
and does not care
that real tears
flow there

THE WAVE THE FLAME
THE CLOUD AND THE LEOPARD
SPEAK TO THE MIND

Watch and watch and follow me
I am all green mimicry
      In my manyness you see
what engenders my beauty

Dancer red and gold with greed
I am that which does not bleed
      On my rising breath be carried
Twine with me and so be freed

Ride with me and hold my mane
I am chimæra the skein
      of everchange that's lily-lain
above the steady mountain

            Go the circle of my cage
I own nothing but my rage
      the black and white of the savage
This singleness may you assuage

THE ENGAGEMENT

When snow
a wing
is folded
over everything

cross
to where
I flow
in the rainbow

when night
a net
dips us
in forget

seek me
in the rock
break
that lock

when blue
my eye
leaks into
a sky

meet me
in the wheel
your thread
I'll feel

and floss
your skin
is what the
spiders spin

I'll come
to where you sink
in the tiger's
blink

when stone
our veins
are parted
chains

and catch you
in the fish
with my strenuous
wish

when prism
sun
bends us
one from one

Find me
in the flake
I will
wake

THE CHARM BOX

As if the knob,
perhaps of porcelain,
of a small calliope
turns around twice:

then a hush,
while the memory
of the dainty fragment
is listened to
by the box itself:

the hermit thrush,
that plain instrument,
not seeming precious,
twice releases
its throb.

This double jewel,
this brief,
lovely jangle
is all there is in it.

One expects the knob
to spin and—in a rush—
a long-looped ornament
of every color to dangle
down the air.

A spoke in there
is not broken.
It's just that stunted
quirk—repeated—

and attention to
the silence in between
that is the amulet
that makes the
charm box work.

The hermit thrush
refuses to be luscious,
to elaborate, to entangle,
to interpret, to defend,
or even to declare a goal.

Only the strict
reiteration of a rarity
from this small calliope,
until it is convinced
its bare beginning
is the end, and the whole.

WAITING FOR *IT*

My cat jumps to the window sill
and sits there still as a jug.
He's waiting for me, but I cannot be
coming, for I am in the room.

His snout, a gloomy V of patience,
pokes out into the sun.
The funnels of his ears expect
to be poured full of my footsteps.

It, the electric moment, a sweet
mouse, will appear; at his gray
eye's edge I'll be coming home
if he sits on the window-ledge.

It is here, I say, and call him
to my lap. Not a hair
in the gap of his ear moves.
His clay gaze stays steady.

That solemn snout says: *It*
is what is about to happen, not
what is already here.

THE WORD "BEAUTIFUL"

Long, glossy caterpillar
with softest feet
of audible and inaudible vowels;

dewberry head so black
it's silver;
nippered lip, and fluent rump;

who moves by the T
at his tifted middle,
a little locomotive hump.

His ripple is felt
by the palm ashamed,
and we are loath to name him;

hairs of his back
a halo's paint
we daren't put round objects any more.

He's tainted,
doomed to sloth, like those
other lunar insects such

as Velvet,
that we must not touch,
or Rose, or Gold.

His destiny—
a myth or moth—still glows
inside the skull,

although his creep is blue,
the untrusted phosphor
of our sleep.

THE POPLAR'S SHADOW

When I was little, when
the poplar was in leaf,
its shadow made a sheaf,
the quill of a great pen
dark upon the lawn
where I used to play.

Grown, and long away
into the city gone,
I see the pigeons print
a loop in air and, all
their wings reversing, fall
with silver undertint
like poplar leaves, their seams
in the wind blown.

Time's other side, shown
as a flipped coin, gleams
on city ground
when I see a pigeon's feather:
little and large together,
the poplar's shadow is found.

Staring at here,
and superposing then,
I wait for when.
What shapes will appear?
Will great birds swing
over me like gongs?
The poplar plume belongs
to what enormous wing?

ORDER OF DIET

1

Salt of the soil and liquor of the rock
is all the thick land's food and mead.
And jaws of cattle grip up
stuffs of pasture for their bellies' need.
We, at table with our knives,
cut apart and swallow other lives.

2

The stone is milked to feed the tree;
the log is killed when the flame is hungry.
To arise in the other's body?
Flank of the heifer we glut, we spend
to redden our blood. Then do we send
her vague spirit higher? Does the grain
come to better fortune in our brain?

3

Ashes find their way to green;
the worm is raised into the wing;
the sluggish fish to muscle slides;
eventual chemistry will bring
the lightning bug to the shrewd toad's eye.
It is true no thing of earth can die.

4

What then feeds on us? On our blood
and delectable flesh: the flood
of flower to fossil, coal to snow,
genes of glacier and volcano,
and our diamond souls that are bent
upward? To what Beast's intent
are we His fodder and nourishment?

DEATH, GREAT SMOOTHENER

Death,
great smoothener,
maker of order,
arrester, unraveler, sifter and changer;
death, great hoarder;
student, stranger, drifter, traveller,
flyer and nester all caught at your border;
death,
great halter;
blackener and frightener,
reducer, dissolver,
seizer and welder of younger with elder,
waker with sleeper
death, great keeper
of all that must alter;
death,
great heightener,
leaper, evolver,
great smoothener,
great whitener!

A CAGE OF SPINES   2

··· *riddling poems* ···

AT
BREAKFAST

Not quite
spherical
White
Oddly closed
and without a lid

A smooth miracle
here in my hand
Has it slid
from my sleeve?

The shape
of this box
keels me oval
Heels feel
its bottom
Nape knocks
its top

Seated
like a foetus
I look for
the dream-seam

What's inside?
A sun?
Off with its head
though it hasn't any
or is all head no body
a
One

Neatly
the knife scalps it
I scoop out
the braincap
soft
sweetly shuddering

Mooncream
this could be
Spoon
laps the larger
crescent
loosens a gilded
nucleus
from warm pap
A lyrical food

Opened
a seamless miracle
Ate a sun-germ
Good

BY MORNING

Some for everyone
   plenty

   and more coming

Fresh   dainty   airily arriving
   everywhere at once

Transparent at first
   each faint slice
   slow   soundlessly tumbling

      then quickly thickly a gracious fleece
      will spread like youth   like wheat
      over the city

Each building will be   a hill
   all sharps made round

      dark worn noisy narrows made still
      wide   flat   clean   spaces

Streets will be   fields
   cars be   fumbling sheep

A deep bright harvest will be seeded
   in a night

By morning we'll be   children
   feeding on manna

      a new loaf on every doorsill

HYPNOTIST

His lair framed beneath the clock
a red-haired beast hypnotic in the room
glazes our eyes and draws us close
with delicious snarls and flickers of his claws
We stir our teacups and our wishes feast
on his cruelty

Throw the Christian chairs to him
a wild child in us cries
Or let us be Daniel bared
to that seething maze his mane
Loops of his fur graze the sill
where the clock's face looks scared

Comfort-ensnared and languorous
our unused daring roused resembles him
fettered on the hearth's stage
behind the iron dogs
He's the red locks of the sun
brought home to a cage

Hunched before his flaring shape
we stir our teacups
We wish he would escape
and loosen in ourselves the terrible
But only his reflection pounces
on the parquet and the stair

WAS WORM

Was worm
swaddled in white

Now tiny queen
in sequin coat
peacockbright
drinks the wind
and feeds
on sweat of the leaves

Is little chinks
of mosaic floating
a scatter
of colored beads

Alighting pokes
with her new black wire
the saffron yokes

On silent hinges
openfolds her wings'
applauding hands

Weaned
from coddling white
to lakedeep air
to blue and green

Is queen

AN EXTREMITY

Roused from napping in my lap
this nimble animal or five-legged star
parts its limbs sprat-wide
See where they glide to focus at their base as spokes of a harp
Blunt and fat the first
sharp-tipped tapping the next
the third authentic and the fourth shy
the least a runt begs pardon for his stature   Why
they're separate beasts I see and not one beast with legs

Or a family of dolls
You could dress the tallest as a boy
Already his sister wears a silver belt
That's a toy-baby by her curled if you put a bonnet on it
Here's agile-joint the pointed the smart wife
Square-head short and papa-perfect sits apart
in dignity a wart at knuckle

Turned over open inner skin is vellum   Here's a map
Five islands spread from the mainland in the fist
Seen flat it's a plain
Forked rivers thread to the wrist
or call them roads the rosy pattern sprawled in an M
Forests are stitched with prick-hatched pine-tree criss-marks
Whorled lines are ploughed land   And
ending each pentacle beach are U-bands of sea-rippled sand

Left one looked at right one writes
Star Harp Beast Family of Five
Map laid live in my lap
Clapped together the two arrive are stated
the poem made extremities mated

SHADOW-MAKER

After a season
apparently sterile he
displays his achievements
   Scale upon layered scale
   frieze upon frieze of animate
   pointed perfect spine-bright

     notes are they?
     gestures for a dance?
     glyphs of a daring alphabet?
       Innumerable intimations
       on one theme
       A primal color haunts the whole design

Shadows aping the shapes
of all his strokes
with inbetweens of dark concavity imply
   an elaboration other than the seen
   flashing intervals of quills of light
   that multiply these forms to a luxury

     These finished feathers
     or pennants
     comblike along their staffs
       hide what they depend on
       like profuse transparent surf
       the basic waves

So his body
stiff and occult
twisted by rocks and years
   patient and awkward
   there beneath
   is hardly noticed

     Bars of solid black
     his acrobatic arms
     peer through as pauses
       In chunks of deeper greener silence
       the denser language of roots
       is voluble and invisible

SEVEN NATURAL SONGS

1   Awoke and stretched in all the bodies
    lofted on sinewy air   Clipped out
    beak-shaped cries and skinned the mist
    from the morning

2   Stood wooden wiggled in earth way under
    A toenail scraped a mammoth's tusk
    Jounced and jittered all these lippy leaves

3   Slicked along meddling with rocks   Tore
    their ears off gradually   Sparkling made
    them hop and holler down a slate-cold throat

4   Humped up sucked in all my thongs
    belly-deep to the roaring core   Recoiled
    for a big yellow bloom   Burst and hurled
    wide open pods of light everywhere

5   Loosened and looled elongate in hammocks
    of blue   Evasive of shape and the eggshell's
    curve   Without taint or tint or substance
    dissolved in fleecy sloth

6   Pricked up out of each pore urgent ambitious
    itching to be even   Scurried and spread
    so all is kept level   Forever unfinished
    my mass fernal mystery   Ants read its roots
    tell its juices to sand

7   Once cloud now all memory my motion
    Amorphous creeping slow as sleep to a full
    black gulping flood   The small five-fingered
    blot enlarged beyond identity   Heavy unslaked
    Still hunting form   The hiding place
    The necessary horror

1 Birds   2 Tree   3 Waterfall   4 Sun
5 Clouds   6 Grass   7 Shadow

TO HER IMAGES

As if the aimed
            heads of swans
            with reaching necks
            their napes curved
            came to their images
To the glozed
            the sleeping surface
            black-white-beamed
            her hands on sinuous arms
            the wrists reared dipped
Dilations of light ran
            rapid and chill
            from the high splints
            on the panel
Lower the fingers
            spanned plunged like bills
            and slower orbits began
            and opened
A kind of dawn awoke
            clean in the bone
            of the ear
            clear lake-lappings
            against the steady
            breasts of swans
Targets in the brain
            were pierced by rays
            glancing from the poises
            of those scarcely plucking
            beaks on the keys'
            reflected pinions
Then prongs ripped
            a heavy element
            strong muscled like whirlpool
            flinching the heart's drumskin
Whips of light across the eyes
            those swans
            and her body dived
In groans as of great
            stones embracing under water
            she came to her images
Then silence a long
            mirror rose upright

FRONTISPIECE

In this book I see your face and in your face
your eyes holding the world and all else besides
as a cat's pupils rayed and wide
to what is before them and what more alive
ticks in the shadows flickers in the waves

Your hair in a slow stream curves
from your listening brow
to your ear shaped like a sea-thing found
in that water-haunted house where murmurs
your chaste-fierce name   The vow

that corners your mouth
compelled you to that deep between words and acts
where they cross as sand with salt
There spills the layered light
your sockets lips and nostrils drank

before they sank
On stages of the sea the years tall
tableaus build   The lighthouse you commanded
the room the oak and mutable Orlando
reoccur as the sea's pages to land's mind   The wall

the steep and empty slate
your cane indented until you laid it as a mark
above where the tide would darken
is written in weed and shell how you were sane
when walking you wrapped your face

in the green scarf
the gray
and then the black
The waves carve your hearse and tomb
and toll your voyage out again again

TWO-PART PEAR ABLE

1. Something Missing

In a country where
every tree is a pear tree
it is a shock to see
one tree
(a pear tree undoubtedly
for its leaves are the leaves
of a pear)
that shows no pears

It is a fairly tall tree
sturdy
capable looking
its limbs strong its leaves glossy
its posture in fact exceptionally
pleasing

but there
among the true pear trees
all of which show pears
the pear tree with no pears
appears (to say the least)
unlikely
and therefore
unlovely

You see
those globes invariably
grow in the trees of that country
There are no other kinds of trees
and pears in the pear trees
are what make them trees
as much
(no even more than)
their leaves
Otherwise they would be named
leaf trees

Pears are what the trees *have*
The leaves are accessory
They are there
to set off the shapes
and colors of the fruits
and shade them
(naturally)
and shelter them
It is as if the trees
were great cool nests for the pears
So that a nest
like the rest (apparently)
but empty

is inconceivable
Like seeing a ghost
or at most a body
without bones

It is a shock
and a pity to see
a pear tree
that can't be
but is

2. *Something Added is Worse*

But in another country
where there
are trees just trees
and no one has ever seen
a fruit tree
of any kind
(much less specifically
a pear tree)
suppose a *pear* tree

(This country must be
entirely imaginary
you say and we agree
The other's unlikely
but could be)

Suppose suddenly
in between leaves
(that are the "fruits" actually)
another sort of a leaf
but differently
shaped and colored
heavier
and depending from a gross
stem were discovered
And then more and more

And finally
it is seen that this tree
is infested with pears
(not yet named of course)
hidden
but obviously
getting bigger
growing there with the leaves

And someone says
How horrible
these leaves are turning into
into *fruits*
(fortuitously
inventing an aggressive
name for it)

There will be
general revulsion won't there?
There will be
demand for expulsion

which could easily
succeed
for the time being

And in that country's
dictionary
it will be
a long while before you see
the word *pear*

DECIDING

Deciding to go on digging doing it
what they said outside wasn't any use
inside hiding it made it get ambitious
like a potato in a dark bin it grew
white grabbers for light
out of its navel-eyes not priding
itself much just deciding
it wasn't true inside what they said
outside those bumps were

All humped alike dumped inside
slumped in burlap said roots are no
good out of ground a fruit's
crazy to want to be a flower besides
it's sin changing the given shape
bursting the old brown skin's
suicide wishing to taste like a tulip
to sip colored light outside thumps
said it isn't right

Deciding to keep on striding
from inside bursting the bin-side
poking out wishes for delicious
opposites turning blind eyes to strong
fingers touching meaning more than
sight the navel scars of weaning
used for something finally deciding
to go on digging doing it

A CAGE OF SPINES *3*

WORKING ON WALL STREET

What's left of the sunset's watered blood
settles between the slabs of Wall Street.
Winter rubs the sky bruise-blue as flesh.
We head down into the subway, glad
the cars are padded with bodies so we
keep warm. Emptied from tall closets
where we work, on the days' shelves
reached by elevators, the heap of us,
pressed by iron sides, dives forward under
the city—parcels shipped out in a trunk.

The train climbs from its cut to the trestle.
Sunset's gone. Those slabs across the murky
river have shrunk to figurines, reflecting
the blush of neon—a dainty tableau, all
pink, on the dresser-top of Manhattan—
eclipsed as we sink into the tunnel.
The train drops and flattens for the long
bore under Brooklyn.

Night, a hiatus hardly real, tomorrow
this double rut of steel will racket us back
to the city. We, packages in the trade
made day after day, will tumble out of
hatches on The Street, to be met by swags
of wind that scupper off those roofs
(their upper windows blood-filled by the sun.)
Delivered into lobbies, clapped into upgoing
cages, sorted to our compartments, we'll be
stamped once more for our wages.

LOOKING UPTOWN

All cars run one way:
toward the point of the wedge
where the sky is pinched
in the meeting of perpendiculars.

Over mats of shadow, through
rents of sun, the cars run
with a sound of ripping cloth
in the gape of the avenue,

and cram where it narrows
far uptown. The metallic back
of something scaly
oozes there in its trap.

Here in the foreground,
gigantic terraces
of stone to left and right,
inlaid with squares of mirror;

and the suede
shadows mimic on cement
angular rhomboids, flat parapets,
so that the cars purr

over wide checkers.
Along the corridor,
the eye, as well, must race,
drawn by a stream

of horizontal threads
fastened to that far
blue slice. At every crossing,
pairs of hooded lights

decide to let the cars
proceed. But in the vise
a glinting lizard pack
strangles, drained of speed,

while the free eye dives on,
true and straight,
up the open vertical,
to swallow space.

TO THE STATUE

The square-heeled boat sets off for the Statue.
People are stuck up tight as asparagus stalks
inside the red rails (ribbons tying the bunch.)

The tips, their rigid heads against the fog,
all yearn toward the Statue; dents of waves
all minimize and multiply to where

she, fifteen minutes afar (a cooky-tin-shaped-
mother-doll) stands without a feature
except her little club of flame.

Other boats pass the promenade. It's exciting
to watch the water heave up, clop the pier,
and even off: a large unsteady belly,

oil-scaled, gasping, then breathing normally.
On the curved horizon, faded shapes of ships,
with thready regalia, cobweb a thick sky.

Nearer, a spluttering bubble over the water
(a mosquito's skeletal hindpart, wings detached
and fused to whip on top like a child's whirltoy)

holds two policemen. They're seated in the air,
serge, brass-buttoned paunches behind glass,
serene, on rubber runners, sledding fog.

Coming back, framed by swollen pilings,
the boat is only inches wide, and flat.
Stalk by stalk, they've climbed into her head

(its bronze is green out there, and hugely spiked)
and down her winding spine into their package,
that now bobs forward on the water's mat.

Soon three-dimensional, colored like a drum,
red-staved, flying a dotted flag,
its rusty iron toe divides the harbor;

sparkling shavings curl out from the bow.
Their heads have faces now. They've been to the Statue.
She has no face from here, but just a fist.
(The flame is carved like an asparagus tip.)

WATER PICTURE

In the pond in the park
all things are doubled:
Long buildings hang and
wriggle gently. Chimneys
are bent legs bouncing
on clouds below. A flag
wags like a fishhook
down there in the sky.

The arched stone bridge
is an eye, with underlid
in the water. In its lens
dip crinkled heads with hats
that don't fall off. Dogs go by,
barking on their backs.
A baby, taken to feed the
ducks, dangles upside-down,
a pink balloon for a buoy.

Treetops deploy a haze of
cherry bloom for roots,
where birds coast belly-up
in the glass bowl of a hill;
from its bottom a bunch
of peanut-munching children
is suspended by their
sneakers, waveringly.

A swan, with twin necks
forming the figure three,
steers between two dimpled
towers doubled. Fondly
hissing, she kisses herself,
and all the scene is troubled:
water-windows splinter,
tree-limbs tangle, the bridge
folds like a fan.

ORNAMENTAL SKETCH WITH VERBS

Sunset runs in a seam
over the brows of buildings
   dropping west to the river,
turns the street to a gilded stagger,
makes the girl on skates,
   the man with the block of ice,
   the basement landlady calling her cat
   creatures in a dream,

scales with salamander-red
   the window-pitted walls,
hairs the gutters with brindled light,
helmets cars and boys on bikes
and double-dazzles
   the policeman's portly coat,
halos the coal truck where
   nuggets race from a golden sled,

festoons lampposts to fantastic trees,
lacquers sooty roofs and pavements,
floats in every puddle
   pinks of cloud,
flamingos all the pigeons,
grands all dogs to chows,
enchants the ash cans into urns
   and fire-escapes to Orleans balconies.

SUNDAY IN THE COUNTRY

No wind-wakeness here. A cricket's creed
intoned to the attentive wood all day.
The sun's incessant blessing. Too much gold
weighs on my head where I lay it in light.
Angels climb through my lashes, their wings
so white, every color clings there. Sky,
deep and accusing in its blue, scrapes
my conscience like a nail. I'm glad
for the gray spider who, with torpid
menace, mounts my shoe; for the skittish
fly with his green ass and orange eyes,
who wades in hairs of my arm to tickle
his belly. Long grass, silky as a monk's
beard, the blades all yellow-beamed.
Corporeal self's too shapeful for this manger.
I'm mesmerized by trumpet sun
funneling hallelujah to my veins.

Until, at the tabernacle's back, a blurt
guffaw is heard. An atheistic stranger calls
a shocking word. That wakes the insurrection!
Wind starts in the wood, and strips the pompous
cassocks from the pines. A black and
impudent Voltairean crow has spoiled
the sacrament. And I can rise and go.

FOREST

The pines, aggressive as erect tails of cats,
bob their tips when the wind freshens.

An alert breath like purring stirs below,
where I move timid over humps of hair,

crisp, shadow-brindled, heaving as if
exhilarated muscular backs felt

the wisps of my walking. Looking to sky,
glaring then closing between the slow

lashes of boughs, I feel observed:
up high are oblong eyes that know,

as their slits of green light
expand, squeeze shut, expand,

that I stand here. Suddenly I go,
flick-eyed, hurrying over fur

needles that whisper as if they weren't dead.
My neck-hairs rise. The feline forest grins

behind me. Is it about to follow?
Which way out through all these whiskered yawns?

NEWS FROM THE CABIN

1

Hairy was here.
He hung on a sumac seed pod.
Part of his double tail hugged the crimson
    scrotum under cockscomb leaves—
      or call it blushing lobster claw, that swatch—
      a toothy match to Hairy's red skullpatch.
Cried *peek!* Beaked it—chiselled the drupe.
His nostril I saw, slit in a slate whistle.
White-black dominoes clicked in his wings.
Bunched beneath the dangle he heckled with holes,
    bellysack soft, eye a brad, a red-flecked
    mallet his ball-peen head, his neck its haft.

2

Scurry was here.
He sat up like a six-inch bear,
    rocked on the porch with me;
    brought his own chair, his chow-haired tail.
Ate a cherry I threw.
Furry paunch, birchbark-snowy, pinecone-brown back,
    a jacket with sleeves to the digits.
Sat put, pert, neat, in his suit and his seat, for a minute,
    a frown between snub ears, bulb-eyed head
    toward me sideways, chewed.
Rocked, squeaked. Stored the stone in his cheek.
Finished, fell to all fours, a little roan couch;
    flurried paws loped him off, prone-bodied,
    tail turned torch, sail, scarf.

3

Then, Slicker was here.
Dipped down, cobalt and turquoise brushes
    fresh as paint. Gripped a pine-tassle,
    folded his flaunts, parted his pointed nib, and scrawled
jeeah! on the air.

Japanned so smooth, his head-peak and all his shaft:
  harsh taunts from that dovey shape, soft tints—
  nape and chin black-splintered, quilltips white-lashed.
Javelin-bird, he slurred his color,
  left his ink-bold word here; flashed off.
Morning prints his corvine noise elsewhere,
  while that green toss still quivers with his equipoise.

4

And Supple was here.
Lives nearby at the stump.
Trickled out from under, when the sun struck there.
Mud-and-silver-licked, his length—a single spastic muscle—
  slid over stones and twigs to a snuggle of roots, and hid.
I followed that elastic: loose
  unicolored knot, a noose he made as if unconscious.
Until my shadow touched him: half his curd
  shuddered, the rest lay chill.
I stirred: the ribbon raised a loop;
  its end stretched, then cringed like an udder;
  a bifid tongue, his only rapid, whirred
  in the vent; vertical pupils lit his hood.
That part, a groping finger, hinged, stayed upright.
Indicated what? That I stood
  in his light? I left the spot.

EARLY MORNING: CAPE COD

We wake to double blue:
an ocean without sail,
sky without a clue
of white.
Morning is a veil
sewn of only two
threads, one pale,
one bright.

We bathe as if in ink,
but peacock-eyed and clear;
a roof of periwink
goes steep
into a bell of air
vacant to the brink.
Far as we can peer
is deep

royal blue and shy
iris, queen and king
colors of low
and high.
Then dips
a sickle wing,
we hear a hinged cry:
taut as from a sling

downwhips
a taunting gull.
And now across our gaze
a snowy hull
appears;
triangles
along its stays
break out to windpulls.

With creaking shears
the bright
gulls cut the veil
in two,
and many a clue
on scalloped sail
dots with white
our double blue.

THE TIDE AT LONG POINT

The sea comes up and the sun goes over
    The sea goes out and the sun falls
The stubby shadow of the lighthouse pales
    stretches to a finger and inches east
The wind lifts from off the sea
    and curries and curries the manes of the dunes
The pipers and the terns skate over
    tweaking the air with their talk
In sky clean as a cat-licked dish
    clouds are sandbars bared by ebbing blue

The hourglass is reversed

The sea comes up and the moon peers over
    The sea goes out and the moon swells
The shadow of the lighthouse thick as a boot
    is swiped by a whiskered beam
The wind licks at the jetty stones
    The pipers and terns hunch on the spit
hiding their necks and stilted feet
    The sky has caught a netful of stars
The moon is a dory trolling them in

The hourglass is reversed

The sea comes up and the moon tips under
    The sea goes out and the sun looms
The sun is a schooner making for harbor
    Shallops of cloud are adrift in the west
The wind gallops the waves to a lather
    and lashes the grass that shines on the dunes
The lighthouse looks at its twin in the water
    The pipers and terns preen on its brow

EXECUTIONS

I walk out on thongs of shadow,
my back to the morning sun,
    the pines' dark quivers running
up along their bow

    of sky: taut
blue about to twang
    with the anguish
of summer shot.

    October's target-mark on every leaf,
on points of dew my shadow rips; light
    pierces wings of jays in flight:
they shout my grief.

    Ring, locusts: murder
is prepared:
    shorn fair pine hair
litters the ground; swords

    already have beheaded
mushrooms: black necks rot
    in these sunny grottos
that sumac, blood-beaded,

    drapes. And ghastly fern
here frightens me—spanned
    like my light-catching hands—
a design for urns.

    By stride escaped to the meadow,
I think that mound, that haul
    of sun a health of yellow still
safe from the killer shadow:

but all is beaten flat; torn
shucks in the flogging place,
    pale corpses surpliced
with light. Then hearse-horns

    of macabre crows
sweep over; gibbet-masks
    they cut on blue. I wade in husks,
in broken shafts of arrows.

THE DAY MOON

The day moon, a half ball of snow vaulting
the mountain, was thrown last night by the level east
from a heavy fist.

Its chunk, of metal, passed the pole among the pelting
stars, one curve sliced, the other cupped
in the upright dark, of charcoal. Looped

the parabola of west, lost weight and glamour,
a plaster socket, kneecap-shaped, or as if hammer-
dented. Porous, marrow-old, dawn tossed

it lower. Shrank in the pink net of the sun, a shell
so light no pitch could give it force. Fell
on cold and solid morning, an almost-ball

rolled by a hard hand. Halts
so, until the day aloft the mountain melts,
softens it, bitten wafer, slips it down.

SPRING UNCOVERED

Gone the scab of ice that kept it snug,
the lake is naked.

Skins of cloud on torn blue:
sky is thin.

A cruelty, the ribs of trees
ribboned by sun's organdy.

Forsythia's yellow, delicate rags,
flip in the wind.

Wind buckles the face of the lake;
it flinches under a smack of shot.

Robbed of stoic frost, grass
bleeds from gaffs of the wind.

Rock, ridging the lake,
unchapped of its snowcloth, quakes.

But autumn fruits upon the water,
plumage of plum, and grape, and pumpkin bills:

Two mallards ride, are sunny baskets;
they bear ripe light.

And a grackle, fat as burgundy,
gurgles on a limb.

His bottle-glossy feathers
shrug off the wind.

HER MANAGEMENT

She does not place, relate, or name
the objects of her hall,
nor bother to repair her ceiling,
sweep her floor, or paint a wall
symmetrical with mountains;

cylindrical her tent
is pitched of ocean on one side
and—rakish accident—
forest on the other.
Granular, her rug

of many marbles, or of roots,
or needles, or a bog—
outrageous in its pattern;
the furniture is pine
and oak and birch and beech and elm;

the water couch is fine.
Mottled clouds, and lightning rifts,
leaking stars, and whole
gushing moons despoil her roof.
Contemptuous of control,

she lets a furnace burn all day,
she lets the winds be wild.
Broken, rotting, shambled things
lie where they like, are piled
on the same tables with her sweets,

her fruits, and scented stuffs.
Her management is beauty.
Of careless silks and roughs,
rumpled rocks, the straightest rain,
blizzards, roses, crows,

April lambs and graveyards,
she *chances* to compose
a rich and sloven manor.
Her prosperous tapestries
are too effusive in design

for our analyses—
we, who through her textures move,
we specks upon her glass,
who try to place, relate and name
all things within her mass.

ANOTHER ANIMAL 1

EVOLUTION

the stone
would like to be
Alive like me

the rooted tree
longs to be Free

the mute beast
envies my fate
Articulate

on this ball
half dark
half light
i walk Upright
i lie Prone
within the night

beautiful each Shape
to see
wonderful each Thing
to name
here a stone
there a tree
here a river
there a Flame

marvelous to Stroke
the patient beasts
within their yoke

how i Yearn
for the lion
in his den
though he spurn
the touch of men

the longing
that i know
is in the Stone also
it must be

the same that rises
in the Tree
the longing
in the Lion's call
speaks for all

oh to Endure
like the stone
sufficient
to itself alone

or Reincarnate
like the tree
be born each spring
to greenery

or like the lion
without law
to roam the Wild
on velvet paw

but if walking
i meet
a Creature like me
on the street
two-legged
with human face
to recognize
is to Embrace

wonders pale
beauties dim
during my delight
with Him

an Evolution strange
two Tongues touch
exchange
a Feast unknown
to stone
or tree or beast

LOVE IS

a rain of diamonds
in the mind

the soul's fruit
sliced in two

a dark spring
loosed at the lips of light

under-earth waters
unlocked from their lurking
to sparkle in a crevice
parted by the sun

a temple
not of stone but cloud
beyond the heart's roar
and all violence

outside the anvil-stunned domain
unfrenzied space

between the grains of change
blue permanence

one short step
to the good ground

the bite into bread again

MORNINGS INNOCENT

I wear your smile upon my lips
arising on mornings innocent
Your laughter overflows my throat
Your skin is a fleece about me
With your princely walk I salute the sun
People say I am handsome

Arising on mornings innocent
birds make the sound of kisses
Leaves flicker light and dark like eyes

I melt beneath the magnet of your gaze
Your husky breath insinuates my ear
Alert and fresh as grass I wake

and rise on mornings innocent
The strands of the wrestler
run golden through my limbs
I cleave the air with insolent ease
With your princely walk I salute the sun
People say I am handsome

HE THAT NONE CAN CAPTURE

comes of own accord to me

The acrobat stride his swing in space
the pole rolled under his instep
catches the pits of his knees
is lipped by his triangled groin
fits the fold of his hard-carved buttocks

Long-thighed tight-hipped he drops
head-down and writhes erect
glazed smooth by speed a twirled top
sits immobile in the void

Gravity outwhipped squeezed like dough
is kneaded to his own design
a balance-egg at the plexus of his bowels
counteracting vertigo

Empty of fear and therefore without weight
he walks a wedge of steeper air
indifferent to the enormous stare
of onlookers in rims of awe below

Drumbeats are solid blocks beneath him
Strong brass horn-tones prolong him
on glittering stilts

Self-hurled he swims the color-stippled height
where nothing but whisks of light
can reach him

At night he is my lover

ANOTHER ANIMAL

Another animal imagine moving
  in his rippling hide
    down the track of the centaur
      Robust inside him his heart siphons unction to his muscles
        proving
          this columnar landscape lives
            Last night's dream
              flinches at the mind's lattice
              transformed into a seam of sunlight on his trunk
            that like a tree
          shimmers in ribbons of shadow
        His mystery the invert cloud engulfs me with the grass

    Imagine another moving
  even as I pass
among the trees that need not shift their feet
  to pierce the sky's academy
    and let go their leaves
      let go
        their leaves
          bright desperate as cries
           and do not cry
            Even as I he breathes
              and shall be breathless
            for the mind-connected pulse
          heaves hurries halts for but two reasons
        Loveless then deathless
      but if loved
    surrendered to the season's summit
    the ice-hood the volcano's hiccough
the empty-orbed zero of eclipse

  The lean track dips together where our feet have pounced
    The rugs the pine boughs gave us glisten clean
      We meet like two whelps at their mother's dugs
        Does the earth trounced here recall
          the hipmarks of another fall
            when dappled animals with hooves and human knees
            coupled in the face of the convulsive spurning
          of other cities and societies?

We are wizards mete for burning
and rush forward to our fate
neighing as when centaurs mate

Unable to imagine until late
in the September wood
that another stood out of God's pocket
straddled between beast and human
now each the other's first stern teacher
learns the A and B against the bitten lips
Our coiled tongues strike the first word
Turned heels our star-crossed hands
kick the mind to its ditch in leaf-mold
Open to joy to punishment in equal part
closed to the next mutation
we lie locked at the forking of the heart

ORGANS

hidden in the hair
the spiral Ear
waits to Suck sound

and sly beneath its
ledge the Eye to Spear
the fish of light

the Mouth's a hole
and yet a Cry for
love for loot

with every stolen
breath the Snoot
Supposes roses

nose tongue fishing
eye's Crouched
in the same hutch

nibbling lips and
funnel's there
in the legs' lair
carnivora of Touch

TO CONFIRM A THING

To confirm a Thing and give thanks
                    to the stars that named me
and fixed me in the Wheel of heaven
                    my fate pricked out in the Boxer's chest
in the hips curled over the Horse
                    Though girled in an apple-pink month
and the moon hornless
                    the Brothers glitter in my wristbones
At ankle and knee I am set astride
                    and made stubborn in love

In the equal Night where oracular beasts
                    the planets depose
and our Selves assume their orbits
          I am flung where the Girdle's double studs
grant my destiny
                    I am the Athletes in that zone
My thighs made marble-hard
                    uncouple only to the Archer
with his diametrical bow
                    who prances in the South
himself a part of his horse
          His gemmed arrow splits the hugging twins

The moon was gelded on that other night as well
                    O his feeble kingdom we will tip over
If our feet traverse the milky way
     the earth's eccentric bead on which we balance
is small enough to hide between our toes
                    its moon a mote that the Long Eye
is hardly conscious of
                              nor need we be

The tough the sensuous Body our belief
                        and fitting the pranks of Zeus
to this our universe
            we are Swans or Bulls as the music turns us
We are Children incorrigible and perverse
                   who hold our obstinate seats
on heaven's carousel
                 refusing our earth's assignment
refusing to descend
                 to beget such trifles of ourselves
as the gibbous Mothers do
              We play in the Den of the Gods
and snort at death

Then let me by these signs
                     maintain my magnitude
as the candid Centaur his dynasty upholds
                 And in the Ecliptic Year
our sweet rebellions
               shall not be occulted but remain
coronals in heaven's Wheel

A LOAF OF TIME

A loaf of time
round and thick
So many layers
ledges to climb
to lie on our
bellies lolling
licking our lips
The long gaze a
gull falling
down the cliff's
table   to coast
the constant
waves   The reach-
ing wave-tongues
lick the table
But slowly grayly
slow as the ocean
is gray beyond
the green   slow
as the sky is high
and out of sight
higher than blue
is white   Around
the table's wheel
unbounded   for
each a meal the
centered mound to
be divided   A
wedge for each
and leisure on
each ledge   The
round loaf thick
we lick our lips
Our eyes gull
down the layered
cliff and ride
the reaching waves
that lick but   slowly
the table's
edge   Then slowly
our loaf   Slowly
our ledge

WHY WE DIE

Saw a grave
upon a hill
and thought
of bones
as still
as sticks
and stones

and thought
that mouldering flesh
is worth
as much as earth

and wondered why
we die

and said
because we want to die
and be as dead
as things that
lacking thought beget
no hope and no regret
No man yet
has dared to stay
within himself
till death
dissolved away

Hunger makes him break the fast
and take a taste of death at last
Who'll forego
the craving
who will be
discoverer of
eternity?

QUESTION

Body my house
my horse my hound
what will I do
when you are fallen

Where will I sleep
How will I ride
What will I hunt

Where can I go
without my mount
all eager and quick
How will I know
in thicket ahead
is danger or treasure
when Body my good
bright dog is dead

How will it be
to lie in the sky
without roof or door
and wind for an eye

With cloud for shift
how will I hide?

MORTAL SURGE

We are eager
We pant
We whine like whips cutting the air
The frothing sea
the roaring furnace
the jeweled eyes of animals call to us
and we stand frozen
moving neither forward nor back

In the breathless wedge between night and dawn
when the rill of blood pauses at the sluice of the heart
either to advance or retreat
the stars stare at us face to face
penetrating even the disguise of our nakedness
daring us to make the upward leap
effortless as falling
if only we relax the bowstring of our will

We seek the slippery flesh of other men
expecting to be comforted
or to be punished
or to be delighted beyond imagined delights
to be made clean
or to be baptized in the cool font of evil

We believe in the meeting of lips
in the converging of glances
that a talisman is given
that we shall arise anew
be healed and made whole
or be torn at last from our terrible womb-twin
our very self

We are loved in the image of the dead
We love in the image of the never-born
We shudder to beget with child
We shudder not to beget with child

We scream in the doorway of our beginning
We weep at the exit gate

We are alone and never alone
bound and never secured
let go and never freed
We would dance and are hurled
would build and are consumed
We are dragged backward by the past
jerked forward by the future

Our earth a bloody clot of the sun's cataclysm
sun a severed limb of a shattered universe
In fission
explosion
In separation
congealment

156

SATANIC FORM

Numerals forkmarks of Satan
Triangles circles squares
hieroglyphs of death
Things invented
abortions smelling of the forge
licked to gruesome smoothness by the lathe
Things metallic or glass
frozen twisted flattened
stretched to agonized bubbles
Bricks beams receptacles vehicles
forced through fire hatched to unwilling form
O blasphemies
Time caught in a metal box
Incongruous the rigid clucking tongue
the needled hands the 12-eyed face
against the open window past which drops the night
like a dark lake on end or flowing hair
Night unanimous over all the city
The knuckled fist of the heart opening and closing
Flower and stone not cursed with symmetry
Cloud and shadow not doomed to shape and fixity
The intricate body of man without rivet or nail
or the terrible skirl of the screw
O these are blessed
Satanic form geometry of death
The lariat around the neck of space
The particles of chaos in the clock
The bottle of the yellow liquor light
that circumvents the sifting down of night
O love the juice in the green stem growing
we cannot synthesize
It corrodes in phials and beakers
evaporates in the hot breath of industry
escapes to the air and the dew
returns to the root of the unborn flower
O Satan cheated of your power

THE GREATER WHITENESS

On winter white
 the dead are gray
  In summer night
   the dead were O so white
    Upon their grief-wet burial day
     the dead were black against the clay
O soiled with grief
 when newly dead
  at foot and head
   in summer's moon-black leaf
    the dead were white
     And in the noon-green
      ghost and stone
       rose clean as light
        and fair as bone
O they were black the heavy dead
 that now are light
  and nothing lack
   But even they
    cannot stay
     O cannot be
      white as that winter purity
On winter white
 the dead are gray

A WISH

Out of an hour I built a hut
  and like a Hindu sat
    immune in the wind of time

From a hair I made a path
  and walked and both
    rock and wilderness became

my space and thoroughfare
  With sorrow for a skin
    I felt no wound

Pleasant power like a nut
    ripened and split within me
      Where there had been wrath

it loosened all the world
  to quiet noonday
    My face in the rock my name

on the wildest tree
  My flesh the heath
    of a peaceful clime

THE KEY TO EVERYTHING

Is there anything I can do
or has everything been done
or do
you prefer somebody else to do
it or don't
you trust me to do
it right or is it hopeless and no one can do
a thing or do
you suppose I don't
really want to do
it and am just saying that or don't
you hear me at all or what?

You're
waiting for
the right person the doctor or
the nurse the father or
the mother or
the person with the name you keep
mumbling in your sleep
that no one ever heard of there's no one
named that really
except yourself maybe

If I knew what your name was I'd
prove it's your
own name spelled backwards or
twisted in some way the one you
keep mumbling but you
won't tell me your
name or
don't you know it
yourself that's it
of course you've
forgotten or
never quite knew it or
weren't willing to believe it

Then there *is* something I
can do I
can find your name for you
that's the key to everything once you'd
repeat it clearly you'd
come awake you'd
get up and walk knowing where you're
going where you
came from

And you'd
love me
after that or would you
hate me?
no once you'd
get there you'd
remember and love me
of course I'd
be gone by then I'd
be far away

A DREAM

I was a god and self-enchanted
I stood in a cabinet in the living wood
The doors were carved with the sign of the lizard
whose eye unblinks on emptiness
whose head turns slower than a tooth grows

I wore a mask of skin-thin silver
My hair was frenzied foam stiffened to ice
My feet gloved in petals of imperishable flowers
were hooves and colder than hammers

I lived by magic
A little bag in my chest held a whirling stone
so hot it was past burning
so radiant it was blinding

When the moon rose worn and broken
her face like a coin endlessly exchanged
in the hands of the sea
her ray fell upon the doors which opened
and I walked in the living wood
The leaves turned bronze and the moss to marble

At morning I came back to my cabinet
It was a tree in the daylight
the lizard a scroll of its bark

RUSTY AUTUMN

Rusty autumn to your breast again I come   Memorial tears
I leave in tarnished spoons of grass
Hold me mother though I am grown and you are old
and burning only for death

Sky my childhood   O familiar blue cobbled with clouds
and misting now as with a cataract
where has father gone   the abundant laughter
our tent and shelter   broad shoulders of the sun?
My dad my tall my yellow-bright ladder of delight

Rusty autumn on your flat breast I lie
and rocks and ragweed my ribs feel in the shaggy field
A blemish on each beam of stubble
and its slanting lash of shadow   These are spears
that were your milk-soft breast I trod in the upright green
Summer's flesh lay all the years between
and hid the bloom of hate
seeded that other time the horizontal world heaved
with my tears   Now too late for planting

O mummied breast O brown mother hold me
though you are cold   and I am grown   grown old

I WILL LIE DOWN

I will lie down in autumn
let birds be flying

Swept into a hollow
by the wind
I'll wait for dying

I will lie inert unseen
my hair same-colored
with grass and leaves

Gather me
for the autumn fires
with the withered sheaves

I will sleep face down
in the burnt meadow
not hearing the sound of water
over stones

Trail over me cloud
and shadow
Let snow
hide the whiteness of my bones

ANOTHER ANIMAL 2

ANY OBJECT

any Object before the Eye
can fill the space can occupy
the supple frame of eternity

my Hand before me such
tangents reaches into Much
root and twig extremes can touch

any Hour can be the all
expanding like a cunning Ball
to a Vast from very small

skull and loin the twin-shaped Cup
store the glittering grainery up
for all the sandy stars to sup

any Single becomes the More
multiples sprout from alpha's core
from Vase of legend vessels of lore

to this pupil dark and wild
where lives the portrait of a Child
let me then be reconciled

germ of the first Intent to be
i am and must be seen to see
then every New descends from me

uncoiling into Motion i
start a massive panoply
the anamolecular atoms fly

and spread through ether like a foam
appropriating all the Dome
of absoluteness for my home

FEEL LIKE A BIRD

feel like A Bird
understand
he has no hand

instead A Wing
close-lapped
mysterious thing

in sleeveless coat
he halves The Air
skipping there
like water-licked boat

lands on star-toes
finger-beak in
feather-pocket
finds no coin

in neat head like
seeds in A Quartered
Apple eyes join
sniping at opposites
stereoscope The Scene
Before

close to floor giddy
no arms to fling
A Third Sail
spreads for calm
his tail

hand better
than A Wing?
to gather A Heap
to count
to clasp A Mate?

or leap
lone-free and mount
on muffled shoulders
to span A Fate?

HORSE AND SWAN FEEDING

Half a swan a horse is
   how he slants his muzzle to the clover
   forehead dips in a leaf-lake
   like she the sweet worm sips
   spading the velvet mud-moss with her beak
His chin like another hoof he plants
   to preen the feathered green
Up now is tossed her brow from the water-mask
With airy muscles black and sleek
   his neck is raised curried with dew
He shudders to the tail delicately
   sways his mane wind-hurried
Shall he sail or stay?
Her kingly neck on her male
   imperturbable white steed-like body
   rides stately away

LION

In the bend of your mouth soft murder
   in the flints of your eyes
   the sun-stained openings of caves
Your nostrils breathe the ordained air
   of chosen loneliness

Magnificently maned as the lustrous pampas
   your head heavy with heraldic curls
   wears a regal frown between the brows

The wide bundle of your chest
   your loose-skinned belly frilled with fur
   you carry easily sinuously pacing on suede paws

Between tight thighs
   under the thick root of your tufted tail
   situated like a full-stoned fruit beneath a bough
   the quiver of your never-used malehood is slung

You pace in dung on cement
   the bars flick past your eyeballs
   fixed beyond the awestruck stares of children
Watching you they remember their fathers
   the frightening hairs in their fathers' ears

Young girls remember lovers too timid and white
   and I remember how I played lion with my brothers
   under the round yellow-grained table
   the shadow our cave in the lamplight

Your beauty burns the brain
   though your paws slue on foul cement
   the fetor of captivity you do right to ignore
   the bars too an illusion

Your heroic paranoia plants you in the Indian jungle
   pacing by the cool water-hole as dawn streaks the sky
   and the foretaste of the all-day hunt
   is sweet as yearling's blood
   in the corners of your lips

SUN

With your masculine stride
    you tread insidious clouds and glide
    to the unobstructed parapet of noon-blue

    ruthless rip through cumulous veils of sloth
    spurn their sly caresses and erect
    an immediate stairway to passion's splendid throne

From yourself you fling your own earth-seed
    and orbits organize in the wombless infinite
    for your discipled planets

    radiant boys
    that imitate your stamping feet
    in the elliptic dance of fire

You are not moon-dependent on desire
    in rotund rhythm leashed to a mineral despot
    like that satellite in female furrow sown

    that white rib plucked from Adam-earth
    but appended still
    eclipsed beneath his dark chest
    writhing to his will

    one-sided shield turned to the urgent tide
    compelled to yield to the night-sky slime
    she that marble-smiling sinks in moss
At dawn rubbed thin a mutilate
    she melts and faints in the cold cloud curd

    while you are up afork the first ringing word
    of potent joy the sharp-tined golden shout
    divine and glistering your beard with dewy flames
    sprinting to the pantheon and your god-like games

STONY BEACH

The sea like Demosthenes' mouth
champs upon these stones
whose many stumblings make him suave
The argument molded monotonously by all his lips
in a parliament of overlappings
is vocal but incomprehensible because never finished

Listen listen there is nothing to learn from the sea
Listen he is lucid in sound only
convinces with broken phrases that wizardly
the waves round out in a rune over riddling stones

Beginning again and again with a great *A*
a garbled alphabet he lisps and groans
The insistent eloquence of echoes
has no omega

SKETCH FOR A LANDSCAPE

a clearing her forehead Brisk
wilderness of hair
retreats from the smooth dancing ground
now savage drums are silent In caves
of shade twin jaguars couch
flicking their tails in restless dream Awake
they leap in unison Asleep they sink
like embers Sloping swards her cheekbones
graduate to a natural throne Two lambs
her nostrils curled back to back Follow
the shallow hollow to her lip-points
stung blossoms or bruised fruits Her
lower lip an opulent orchard Her spiral smile
a sweet oasis both hot and cool

soft in center swollen a bole of moss
hiding white stones and a moist spring
where lives a snake so beautiful and shy His
undulant hole is kept a slippery secret A cleft
between the cliff-edge and her mouth we drop
to the shouldered foothills down the neck's
obelisk and rest In the valley's scoop
velvet meadowland

CAFE TABLEAU

Hand of the copper boy
pours tea   deft wrist square fist
salmon-satin-lined

Dark-muscled dancers among porcelain
twined   his fingers and long thumb

He stands dumb in crisp white coat
his blood in heavy neck-vein
eloquent   its flood plunges
to each purple nail   emanates
male electrons

His pupils conscienceless as midnight skies
between the moon-whites of his eyes   avoid
tea-sipper's naked shoulder
diamond-cold her throat

That she is female his broad nostrils
have denied   like figs dried when green
her breasts shrivel in the refusal
of his stare

His thigh athletic slender   retreats
behind her chair   in his hips
nothing tender   ancestral savagery
has left him lion-clean

Furtive beneath mental hedges
she sees   feels his bare wrist square fist
her boneless hand creeps up the crisp sleeve
higher   she squeals and finds the nipples
of his hairless chest

The copper boy's white coat
become a loincloth she unwinds   he wades
into the pool of her stagnant desire

THE GARDEN AT ST. JOHN'S

Behind the wall of St. John's in the city
  in the shade of the garden the Rector's wife
    walks with her baby a girl and the first
      its mouth at her neck seeking and sucking
        in one hand holding its buttocks its skull
          cupped by the other her arms like a basket
            of tenderest fruit and thinks as she fondles
              the nape of the infant its sweat is like dew
                like dew and its hair is as soft as soft
                  as down as the down in the wingpits of angels

The little white dog with the harlequin eye
  his tail like a thumb feet nimble as casters
    scoots in the paths of the garden's meander
      behind the wall of St. John's in the city
        a toy deposed from his place in her arms
          by this doll of the porcelain bone
            this pale living fruit without stone

She walks where the wrinkling tinkling fountain
  laps at the granite head of a monk
    where dip the slippery noses of goldfish
      and tadpoles flip from his cuspid mouth
      A miracle surely the young wife thinks
        from such a hard husband a tender child
          and thinks of his black sleeves on the hymnbook
            inside the wall of St. John's in the city
              the Ah of his stiff mouth intoning Amen
                while the organ prolongs its harmonious snore

Two trees like swans' necks twine in the garden
  beside the wall of St. John's in the city
    Brooding and cool in the shade of the garden
      the scrolled beds of ivy glitter like vipers
        A miracle surely this child and this garden
          of succulent green in the broil of the city
            she thinks as setting the bird-cries apart
              she hears from beneath the dark spirals of ivy
                under the wall of St. John's in the city
                  the rectal rush and belch of the subway
                    roiling the corrugate bowels of the city
                    and sees in the sky the surgical gleam
                      of an airplane stitching its way to the West
                    above the wall of St. John's in the city
                    ripping its way through the denim air

SPRING IN THE SQUARE

Tree trunks intercept the eye
that swoops like a bird through zigzags of green
At far end of the pupil's tunnel
beads of tiny taxis roll
People move like scissored marionettes

Beneath the eyelid's awning
benches slump Sunday sitters
A yawn goes mouth to mouth
Old necks slacken in the sun
Tranced fingers fold black headlines
that swim like giddy bugs
in the great goblet of light

Shadow-and-sun-interbraided
children in pendulous swings
rise loose-kneed and fall
and rise loose-kneed and fall
flashing like watchfobs

The stateman's statue all
winter unmoved by snow
listens in ponderous surprise to summer's bugle

This the moment of released leaves
Innumerable green hands uncurl their puckered palms
Irrepressible grass bristles
from the city's horny hide

HORSES IN CENTRAL PARK

Colors of horses like leaves or stones
or wealthy textures
liquors of light

The skin of a plum that's more than ripe
sheathes a robust
cloven rump

Frosty plush of lilies
for another's head
ears and nostrils funneled are their cones

Of sere October leaves
this gaunt roan's hide
freckled dun and red

Here's a mole-gray back
and darker dappled haunch
tail and forelock mauve like smoke

This coal-colored stallion
flake of white on his brow
is slippery silk in the sun

Fox-red bay
and buckskin blond as wheat
Burgundy mare with tassled mane of jet

Sober chestnut burnished
by his sweat
to veined and glowing oak

Seal-brown mustang
with stocking-feet
Pinto in patched and hooded domino

Naked palomino
is smooth peeled willow
or marble under water or clean morning snow

BOY IN CANOE

In pod-shaped canoe
on the spanking lake
he propels his cradle
through uterine blue
his arms tatooed with
Grace & Force
the scoop of his long chest
Light & Strong
as the shell

Yellow his head
as if pollen-dusted
Stern-innocent his eyes
are turned to the fierce
sun's shield
unmindful of Medusas he must
pierce or yield to
voyage done

Between his thighs
like a young frog
in a loose fist
precious lies his genital
and pulsing in their
pouches wait
the little gold grains
of giant's teeth
to burrow into Dark & Wet
at summer's end
at the lake's bend

THE PLAYHOUSE

Here is the playhouse of weather-faded white
Trees like legs of elephants stamp 'round it
in the mossy light after rain
It sits on a knoll   It's chimney is red
Troll-headed weeds press against the pane

A rabbit could hop the tidy picket fence
but the gate is locked beneath the little wicket
Stooping you can peer like a marionette master
into a room with a table and chair   a sofa in the corner
with antimacassar   a hearth a scuttle and broom

The child is at the table bent above her game
The fire stretches in the grate
With doll-round eyes intent and oranged by the flame
she plays a little black machine
with clever buttons that she taps

spelling out her name perhaps   And now the plaything
is a square of cloth upon a rack   the child a boy
in one hand a plate where colored knobs are stuck
in the other something like a wand
with which he gambles   It's a game of luck

or magic   Like a stage the playhouse
or like a fairy book improbable and charming
Each time you look inside you see a different play
Is that a toy piano he's diddling on today?
Odd how they never see you watching

Now she's making up a dance
He's buffeting a lump of mud into a fancied shape
Out in the giant wood birds with beaks agape
listen   In gauzy trance the deer stand still
They sense there's something queer

Is the playhouse really here you wonder
and what's it to do with you?
There's a spatter of rain   there's thunder
In a flick of lightning will you see what it means
or will it disappear?

Are the children real if the forest is?
On the path that leads to the playhouse on its knoll
next time you come will there be a hole
matted with weeds?   What if it's you who's missing
or at least invisible   too large a beast for the landscape?

Your feet do not impress the moss
or make a sound among the plodding trees
impassive in the rain   Turn 'round
Can you see the playhouse?   No it's gone
Now do you feel the loss and the puzzling pain?

BIG–HIPPED NATURE

Big-hipped nature bursts forth the head of god
from jungle clots of green
from pelvic heave of mountains
On swollen-breasted clouds he fattens and feeds
He is rocked in the crib of the sea

Stairways of the inner earth he crawls
and coos to us from the caves
The secret worms miracle his veins
Myriads of fish embellish his irridescent bowels
In multiple syllables the birds
inscribe on air his fledgling words

Swift and winding beasts with coats of flame
serpents in their languor black and blind
in the night of his dark mind express
his awe and anger his terror and magicness

Wherever we look his eye lies bottomless
fringed by fields and woods
and tragic moons
magnify his pupils with their tears

In fire he strides
Within the waterfall
he twines his limbs of light
Clothed in the wind and tall
he walks the roofs and towers
Rocks are all his faces
flowers the flesh of his flanks
His hair is tossed with the grasses everywhere
Stained by the rainbow every shell
roars his whispered spell

When sleep the enormous shadow of his hand descends
our tongues uncoil a prayer
to hush our ticking hearts our sparrow-like fear
and we lie naked within his lair
His cabalistic lightnings play upon us there

GREEN RED BROWN AND WHITE

Bit an apple on its red
side   Smelled like snow
Between white halves broken open
brown winks slept in sockets of green

Stroked a birch white as a thigh
scar-flecked smooth as the neck
of a horse   On mossy pallets green
the pines dropped down
their perfect carvings brown

Lost in the hairy wood
followed berries red
to the fork   Had to choose
between green and green   High

in a sunwhite dome a brown bird
sneezed   Took the path least likely
and it led me home   For

each path leads both out and in
I come while going   No to and from
There is only here   And here
is as well as there   Wherever
I am led I move within the care
of the season
hidden in the creases of her skirts
of green or brown or beaded red

And when they are white
I am not lost   I am not lost then
only covered for the night

AN OPENING

close to sleep an Opening
   what was wall
   to the light-filled eye
   or panel fingertips could find no groove in
   slides apart   the Box
   of Now of Me of only Here unlocks

at once in a landscape limitless and free
   all that my Eye encircles I become
   trees ponds pastures   bullocks grazing there
   silks of my Skin strands of my Hair
   waters of my body glittering

Then and Forever are my two hands spread
   forgotten by each other   my Head
   an orchard where in noons of ebony
   in the white night are mated East and West
   and polar fruits and flowers from the sea
   are harvested

together   now I know I have been Hooded
   on rails my sight has run
   to its Horizon where the future spun
   or tapered to the gray Thread
   hooked in the past   and these have dropped away
   like markers lost in corridors of Snow
   I am an eye that without socket looks
   on all sides above below

where is Wakeness then?   rigid these wires
   and joints and jerky stilts when Upright I
   am stretched in the frame again   the sky
   a Lid I cannot pry   the air
   a tissue of whispers I cannot tear

when narrowed utterly   the final Blind
   box of sleep clapped shut
   unhinged from sight then will I find
   within the pupil of the total deep the Wide
   doorway to fields of bright
   Bristles of the sun to be my hide